Homeland Security & Terrorism

THREAT, INCIDENT & AFTERMATH

JIBEY ASTHAPPAN
University of New Haven

Kendall Hunt
publishing company

Cover image © Shutterstock.com

Kendall Hunt
publishing company

www.kendallhunt.com
Send all inquiries to:
4050 Westmark Drive
Dubuque, IA 52004-1840

Copyright © 2017 by Kendall Hunt Publishing Company

ISBN 9781524922467

Published in the United States of America

BRIEF CONTENTS

CONTENTS

ABOUT THE AUTHOR

Dr. Asthappan began his career in 1999 as an Explosive Ordnance Disposal Technician for the U.S. Air Force. Following the 9/11 attacks, he was deployed with some of the first troops in Operation Enduring Freedom. He served as a bomb technician to protect civilians and military targets from improvised explosive devices (IEDs) as well as chemical, biological, and nuclear weapons.

Dr. Asthappan has conducted extensive research on counterterrorism and crisis management. While obtaining a PhD in Justice, Law, and Society from American University, Dr. Asthappan completed a study that would later be published as a book: *Stealing Their Thunder: The Effectiveness of Military Force in Deterring Terrorism*. Currently, Dr. Asthappan teaches courses on homeland security, criminal justice, terrorism, criminology, cybercrime, and network security at the University of New Haven.

Courtesy University of New Haven

OVERVIEW

Counter-terrorism literature has experienced an incredible increase in the quantity and quality of books that review the topic. In colleges around the country, Homeland Security and Terrorism is taught with a wide array of topics covered and spectrum of expected outcomes of students. Some teachers focus on the history of terrorism while others focus on the theoretical underpinnings. Few address what the real world needs from responders to policy-makers—skills to manage the risk of terrorism from inception, social counter-culture, to managing the risk of a terrorist event. This book is not only an effort to fill in a gap in the literature, but also it is an effort to fill the gap in education. This book is written by a practitioners-turned educator, who worked in the field as Explosive Ordnance Disposal and who wants to teach students how critical thinking and problem solving is the keystone to counter-terrorism. The author transitioned from practitioners to theorist and an educator who seeks a long-term solution to a complex problem.

The book is organized to offer a historical and theoretical foundation. This approach assists students in understanding the underlying motivations for terrorism. It is from this perspective that terrorism prevention plans can be best understood. The book then transitions to counterterrorism strategies. The emphasis chapters one to five are designed to give the student a foundation of what is being done to address terrorism and protect a population. Finally, the incident and recovery after an incident becomes the focus of the chapters six to nine. The student learns how to identify, organize, and mitigate risk after an incident has occurred. Chemical, biological, nuclear, and active shooter threats are reviewed from a pragmatic perspective. Students learn about each threat and gain an understanding of how to mitigate the threat. Tabletop exercises are used to emulate what practitioners do in the real world to prepare for a terrorist event. The process of moving from factual knowledge to an actionable process is an important step for students who wish to work in the field of counterterrorism.

CHAPTER 1

Introduction to Homeland Security and Terrorism

INTRODUCTION TO TERRORISM

The study of homeland security and terrorism is interdisciplinary in nature. The motivations of terrorists are studied in the fields in psychology, political science, criminal justice, and sociology. The *actions* of terrorists are studied in biology, chemistry, physics, and electrical engineering. The immediate response to terrorism is also multidisciplinary. Incident planning and emergency

© Nazar Gonchar/Shutterstock.com

A memorial for the victims of the November 13, 2015 Paris terror attacks.

response is a growing area of study that involves studies in psychology, criminal justice, and engineering. Continued professionalism in the field will offer better services to victimized populations. Finally, policymaking aimed to prevent and thwart a terrorist attack involves all the above-mentioned areas of study. This chapter will review the functions of local, state, and federal entities in preventing terrorist attacks and mitigating the loss after an incident.

LEARNING OUTCOMES

1. Identify the variety of entities that make up the Intelligence Community (IC)
2. Identify the duties of the various jobs that make up community tasked with deterring and responding to a mass emergency
3. Comprehend how the variety of jobs work together to form a response to an undesirable event

Jobs in Counterterrorism

Background Checks

FBI: Most Professional Staffs' jobs within the division fall into the category of Intelligence Analyst, Technical Information Specialist, or Financial Analyst, and involve working with various entities within the Intelligence Community (IC). There are also many opportunities for entry-to upper-level administrative, professional, and technical positions that support many programs within the division.

Military Functions

The military offers a plethora of job opportunities in the area of homeland security and counterterrorism. Duties and objectives of the job varies greatly. Officers and enlisted may have the same job code, but their day-to-day duties are far different. Officers generally make or assist in making decisions for the units that they command while enlisted are usually tasked with carrying out the tasks to meet the mission's goals. National guard members are controlled by the state and are usually called upon when a natural disaster strikes. Keep in mind that all military members are tasked with the same overall purpose—to win wars. Helping people can be part of the job and even part of a member's duties, but ultimately, helping people comes secondary to winning a war.

Federal Law Enforcement

- FBI Police (https://www.fbijobs.gov/126.asp)

As part of the Security Division, FBI Police Officers provide protective security to FBI personnel, facilities, and information; and perform law enforcement duties in and around some of the FBI's most important facilities. The primary mission of the FBI Police is to deter terrorist attacks with the visible presence of a well-trained, well-equipped, professional police force; and to protect the FBI from criminal acts and unauthorized access. All FBI Police Officers receive extensive training and must become proficient with a firearm. Work schedule flexibility is essential. Also, all FBI Police Officers must agree to remain in the FBI Police Officer position, at the location to which he/she is assigned, for a minimum of 2 years.

- FBI Special Agent (https://www.fbijobs.gov/11.asp)

FBI Special Agents are responsible for conducting sensitive national security investigations and for enforcing over 300 federal statutes. As an FBI Special Agent you may work on matters including terrorism, foreign counterintelligence, cybercrime, organized crime, white-collar crime, public corruption, civil rights violations, financial crime, bribery, bank robbery, extortion, kidnapping, air piracy, interstate criminal activity, fugitive and drug-trafficking matters, and other violations of federal statutes.

- CIA Police Officer

The mission of the Security Protective Service (SPS) is the protection of Agency's personnel, facilities, and information through the enforcement of Federal Laws and Agency Regulations. The SPS provides a full range of high-quality security/police services through a variety of specialty units and fixed posts where officers routinely work 8-hour shifts to include weekends/holidays and may be directed to work overtime. Premium pay is compensated for working Sundays, nights, and holidays. Career enhancements can be obtained by pursuing assignments in the areas of: threat management, K-9, explosive ordnance detection, HAZMAT, security operations, and court liaison.
-Job is in Washington DC. Five-year minimum commitment.

- CIA Protective Agent

Typical duties of the Protective Agent include deploying worldwide to perform sensitive operations in support of protective requirements. Protective Agents are consistently called upon to deploy and participate in training and operational assignments and are expected to work long hours and deploy for periods from 45 to 60 days in length. The amount of yearly travel is extensive, and interested candidates should expect to deploy as scheduled.

- DHS Customs and Border Protection

On duty at one of our nation's international airports, seaports, or land border crossings. Defense against terrorist intrusion as well as criminal activities, such as drug smuggling, money laundering, undocumented entry of individuals, weapons trafficking, smuggling of prohibited goods, and a host of customs violations.

- Federal Emergency Management Agency (FEMA)

Not a full-time position available until after 1 year of continuous service. There are also temporary local hires, 120 days, which can be continued for up to 1 year. Reservists, mostly on call, temporary, may interview disaster victims, conduct and verify damage assessments, etc.

- Secret Service Special Agent

Two missions are protections and criminal investigation. Can be assigned anywhere in the world. Protect current and past presidents and their families as well as visiting heads of foreign states or governments and their families, etc. Investigations are mostly money based: counterfeiting, all kinds of fraud, false documents, money laundering, as well as

© Ververidis Vasilis/Shutterstock.com

Secret Service Special Agents protect the President.

computer-based attacks on nation's financial structure.

• NSA Police Officer

Help protect those who keep our nation safe with a career in Security at NSA. NSA has an ongoing requirement for personnel to serve as NSA Police Officers on its complexes in and around Fort Meade, Maryland. Qualified individuals are encouraged to apply for these positions offering exceptional training and the opportunity to serve your country as an employee of one of the most unique and respected agencies in the federal government. Primary responsibilities: Counterterrorism and force protection, asset protection, and pedestrian and vehicular access control; response and mitigation of security, medical, and fire emergencies; critical incident management; enforcement of laws and regulations relative to the protection of NSA assets; vehicle, facility, and material security inspections; firearms training and range management; and Patrol of NSA property.

• NCIS Special Agent

Will most likely be working abroad. Not required to be in the navy/military to be a special agent, but preferred. Includes training on subjects ranging from death investigations to crime scene processing, domestic security, unarmed self-defense, and critical incident stress debriefing to multimonth programs on technical surveillance countermeasures, polygraph, procurement fraud, protective service, and year-long graduate programs in forensic science, foreign counterintelligence, and language studies.

State Police/Law Enforcement

• State Police Officers

Highway patrol, taking people into custody/fingerprinting/booking them, etc. Job description may depend on the amount of time in department.

• State Detectives

Usually requires person to be a police officer before they can get detective job. Different kinds of detectives, homicide, sex crimes, etc., interview suspects, witnesses, etc. Work closely with the crime scene unit. Investigate crimes to try to piece together how they occurred.

Local Police

Supposed to ensure safety of citizens and their property as well as enforce any laws that may be broken. Also responsible for responding to emergency situations. Usually, depending on the town, most of the time is spent in a patrol car. Writing reports is a huge part of the job.

Emergency Management

Local police officers protect citizens and property.

- Office of Emergency Management Watch Command Supervisor

Duties include: supervising the on-duty staff of Watch Command; coordinating with the Director of Field Response to monitor and update the status of response personnel and assets; ensuring adequate staffing for upcoming tours of duty; ensuring that communication about public safety or public health incidents that adversely impact the city and require a multiagency response is properly processed including, but not limited to, confirming the scope and nature of incidents, ensuring that agency notifications are performed, analyzing information from multiple sources, preparing reports for dissemination to executive staff and senior officials of the city, and interfacing with the city's Emergency Operations Center (EOC); supporting communications in the field at large events or incidents; performing staff training; assisting in drills and exercises; and other duties as assigned by the Deputy Commissioner of Operations or the Director of Watch Command.

- Office of Emergency Management Security Engineer

Assist the agency with security-related technical support of servers, SQL, VMware, Exchange, desktops, laptops, mobile services, applications, and all related technology. Support includes specification, installation, and testing of computer systems and peripherals within established policies, standards, and guidelines. Activities require interaction with application software and operating systems to diagnose and resolve unique problems. The position utilizes one-on-one consultancy to end users. The position's responsibilities require independent analyses, communication, and problem solving.

- FEMA Emergency Management Officer

Responds to a mass emergency or disaster and creates a plan to mitigate the risk. The individual will coordinate with partners in the community, including public and private entities, in order to manage and reduce the risk from an emergency or disaster.

- FEMA External Affairs Specialist

Maintain visibility regarding public and internal communications; coordinate routine and special communications; ensure accurate, useful, timely, synchronized, targeted communication; and provide continuous messaging to meet the needs of the situation.

- FEMA Program Specialist

Follow predeployment and check-in procedures; follow check-out procedures; complete ongoing administrative procedures; establish and maintain positive and ethical behaviors during interpersonal, intra-agency, and interagency interactions; help resolve problems/issues and make effective decisions; prepare written reports and other documents; communicate orally with others to exchange and clarify information; and exhibit an understanding of relevant safety and security procedures.

- FEMA Program Analyst

Coordinates and responds to high-level assignments and issues. Prepares presentations, reports, and findings; makes recommendations; Arranges for; and Participates in the implementation of recommendations accepted and approved. Provides analytical support to senior staff in reviewing, analyzing, and editing various documents, including correspondence, doctrine, policy, legislation, General Accounting Office, and/or Inspector General reports. Formulates recommendations to senior managers based on knowledge of current issues, legislation, and regulations. Researches and coordinates directorate responses and provides input, as required, to questions from Congress, the Department of Homeland Security (DHS), and the White House. Participates in development of preparedness plans and other multiyear planning documents and management improvement activities to support strategic planning. Monitors and follows up on tasks assigned to senior managers. Assists with organizing and participating in meetings and conferences that may involve Interagency partners.

- FEMA Emergency Communications Dispatcher

Receives, processes, and relays emergency and routine communications via radio, telephone, computer, alarm device, and teletype, and dispatches police, fire, and emergency medical services (EMS). Prepares required documentation and performs operator maintenance on communications equipment. Performs related functions.

- FEMA Regional Security Advisor

Security consultants conduct tests on a current system to determine weak areas, which are vulnerable to an attack. After testing, they prepare reports which determine what could be done to better protect.

- FEMA Plans and Operations Specialist

Typically responsible for allocating resources, planning schedules, managing daily operations, and training staff.

Fire Science/Arson Investigation

- DOD Fire Protection Engineer

They study the causes of fires and how architecture and design influence the prevention and suppression of fires. They inspect building plans and structures to evaluate which fire detection, fire alarm, and fire-fighting equipment will keep occupants and property from catastrophic damage.

- Department of the Interior Fire Management Specialist

Provide specialized guidance and advice in development, management, and implementation of prescribed fire, hazardous fuels reduction, and fire planning programs and policies. The position requires knowledge of fuels management, fire behavior, fire regimes, fuel and ecological factors that determine fire-severity, etc.

- Department of Agriculture Fire Management Officer

Responsible for providing leadership and program direction for the unit's fire and aviation management program. The incumbent is responsible for coordinating the development of short-and long-range fire management program plans, fire management activities on the unit, and integrating the unit's fire management program with other disciplines and inter-agency partners to achieve goals consistent with the Federal Wildland Fire Policy and agency manual direction.

- DOA Forestry Technician

Perform duties such as: suppression of wildfires as a crew member on an engine, helitack, or hotshot team; maintain facilities in campgrounds, provide visitors with information about a locality, or explain fire, safety, and sanitation regulations; clear or repair some of the Forest Service's 100,000 miles of trails, or help construct a new trail; help protect a wilderness area by monitoring uses and enforcing regulations; plant trees or shrubs to rehabilitate a damaged site, or to stabilize a slope; analyze tree stands for growth conditions, disease, and insect infestations; improve timber stands as a member of a tree-planting or thinning crew or of a group collecting and classifying cones by species or condition; "cruise" prospective sale areas to determine species, types, and qualities of timber; select and mark trees to be cut, as well as those to be preserved for natural reseeding or as wildlife habitats; Interpret aerial photos to identify types of timber and habitat; inventory sites for prescribed fire/fuels management activities; and inspect recreation and timber sale sites or reforestation activities for compliance with special permits.

- DOA Forest Fire Management Officer

Manage and care for more than 193 million acres of our nation's most magnificent lands, conduct research through a network of forest and range experiment stations and the Forest Products Laboratory, and provide assistance to State and private forestry agencies.

Responsible for providing leadership and program direction for the unit's fire and aviation management program. Responsible for coordinating the development of short-and long-range fire management program plans, fire management activities on the unit.

- DOD Explosives Investigator

Conducts examinations of evidence associated with bombing matters.

- DOE Fire Protection Engineer

Performs duties related to advising on, administering, supervising, or performing research or other professional and scientific work in the investigation or development of fire protection projects. Assignments may include design, construction, inspection, testing, operation, maintenance of firefighting or fire protection apparatus, appliances, devices and systems, or the testing of fire resistant materials.

- ATF Fire Engineer

They conduct fire experiments to recreate fire scenes and identify fire dynamics characteristics to assist with investigations. They can demystify topics such as flashover, smoke behavior, and fire protection system operations to provide a better understanding to firefighters. In the community, the FPE can enhance the public's perception of fire safety and fire protection systems, particularly with regard to residential smoke alarms and the heated battle over residential sprinkler legislation.

Intelligence

- FBI Intelligence Analyst (https://www.fbijobs.gov/121.asp)

They are on the frontline of protecting America's national security. They piece together disparate bits of information to form integrated views on issues of national security and public safety by: utilizing language, cultural, and historical knowledge to combat international threats by working within specifically defined geographical and/or functional areas (e.g., China program, Weapons of Mass Destruction program, al-Qa'ida program, etc.); discover domestic threats by leveraging local and national intelligence databases, analyzing intelligence collected in the field offices, and developing fact-based conclusions and intelligence reports; shaping intelligence policies by maintaining extensive networks and partnering with local, national, and international contacts within the intelligence and law enforcement communities, and leverage it to prepare briefings, reports, and communications for senior FBI executives and other IC and Law Enforcement entities.

- FBI Information Technology (https://www.fbijobs.gov/122.asp)

They build, operate, and maintain the FBI's IT enterprise. This includes: developing the FBI's IT strategic plan and operating budget; developing and maintaining the FBI's technology assets; and providing technical direction for the reengineering of FBI business processes. IT professionals also work in support of FBI investigations and provide state-of-the-art identification and information services to our local, state, federal, and international criminal justice partners.

- FBI Linguists (https://www.fbijobs.gov/124.asp)

They play a vital role in the translation, transcription, reporting, and analysis of materials with national security ramifications. They investigate crimes such as terrorism, foreign counterintelligence, organized crime,

FBI IT professionals provide investigation support.

air piracy, interstate criminal activity, public corruption, financial crime, bribery, civil rights violations, kidnapping, drug trafficking, and more.

- FBI Investigative and Surveillance Specialists (https://www.fbijobs.gov/127.asp)

They perform investigative support functions through physical surveillance operations. They support Foreign Counterintelligence and/or Counterterrorism investigations, and gather intelligence information of investigative interest. Investigative Specialists are responsible for all aspects of surveillance operations from planning through execution. Their responsibilities also include the collection, analysis, and dissemination of intelligence data gathered during surveillance operations.

- FBI Applied Science, Engineering, and Technology (https://www.fbijobs.gov/123.asp)

Typical challenges range from how to identify a potential terrorist based on a partial fingerprint, to how to listen in to the conversations of a suspected criminal, and how to perform lawfully authorized searches.

- Computer Science
- Forensic Science
- Explosives/Incendiary Devices
- Telecommunications
- Cryptography

- CIA Analytic Methodologist

They provide statistical, operations research, econometric, mathematical, geospatial modeling, or survey support to Agency analysis, and communicate their findings via a broad range of written intelligence products and verbal presentations.

- CIA Counterintelligence Threat Analyst

They identify, monitor, and assess the efforts of foreign intelligence entities who attempt to collect sensitive national security information on U.S. persons, activities, and interests, including the threats posed by emerging technologies to U.S. operations and interests. They support U.S. policymakers with strategic assessments and provide tactical analysis and advice for operations.

- NSA Cryptanalysis

Cryptanalysis is the analytic investigation of an information system with the goal of illuminating hidden aspects of that system. It encompasses any systematic analysis aimed at discovering features in, understanding aspects of, or recovering hidden parameters from an information system.
—No specific major required.

- NSA Intelligence Analysis

The process of generating intelligence from data and information derived from foreign signals. Intelligence analysts are the Agency's professionals whose research, analysis, and presentation of findings provide the most complete possible signals intelligence (SIGINT) picture. SIGINT is used by U.S. policymakers, military commanders, and other IC organizations to assist in Executive Branch decisions and actions.

- NCIS—Cyber Specialist

They utilize advanced cyber technologies and methodologies to process, identify, and present electronic data of intelligence or evidentiary value. In applying expertise in dissecting and analyzing almost any form of electronic communications, memory storage device or network system, the Cyber Department plays a critical role in core NCIS missions: combating terrorism, counterintelligence, and general criminal investigations.

- Computer Scientist
  Develop innovative and specialized tools, analyze and write code, install network devices, and conduct testing of software and equipment. They share their expertise and insights by providing technical assistance to other Cyber personnel within the IC, not only in the United States, but assist other countries dealing with similar challenges of data and data systems attacks.

- Investigative Computer Specialist
  Primarily focus on computer forensics and other storage devices and provide rapid response to computer intrusion incidents.

- Cyber Intelligence Analysts
  Specialize in review of Cyber data for items of potential intelligence value and apply their expertise to produce actionable intelligence products.

- NCIS—Intelligence Specialist

They collect and assess intelligence from a number of sources, such as national databases, domestic/foreign media publications, and contacts with peers in other intelligence and law enforcement agencies. They prepare intelligence reports, brief senior DON policy and decision makers, and closely coordinate and support NCIS counterterrorism, counterintelligence, and criminal investigations and operations.

- Computer Emergency Response Team (CERT)

They partner with government, industry, law enforcement, and academia to develop advanced methods and technologies to counter large-scale, sophisticated cyber threats. CERT works closely with the DHS to meet mutually set goals in areas such as data collection and mining, statistics and trend analysis, computer and network security, incident management, insider threat, software assurance, and more. The results of this work include exercises, courses, and systems that were designed, implemented, and delivered to DHS and its customers as part of the SEI's mission to transition SEI capabilities to the public and private sectors and improve the practice of cybersecurity.

- DHS Security Specialist

They are trained in emergency management, preparedness, and response. These specialists can work for governmental agencies or private corporations. A main component of a homeland security specialist's job description is to protect local, state, and federal infrastructure in the event of disaster or terrorist attack. Homeland security specialists might also be trained in other primary fields, including law enforcement or EMS. Homeland security specialists usually work within a team of other security specialists.

- DHS Information Security Officer

They address cybersecurity issues and challenges and share expertise regarding the implementation of key cybersecurity capabilities in their respective enterprises. The Advisory Councils also serve as a key channel for CISOs to be briefed on available DHS and Federal Network Resilience (FNR) cybersecurity service offerings. The mission of DHS's FNR branch is to improve the security posture of the Federal civilian enterprise, and this two-way dialogue serves to inform and share pertinent ideas with agency stakeholders and DHS alike.

- Department of State Foreign Affairs Officer

Mission is to promote peace, support prosperity, and protect American citizens while advancing the interests of the United States abroad. You will be asked to serve at one of any of the more than 270 embassies, consulates, and other diplomatic missions in the Americas, Africa, Europe and Eurasia, East Asia and Pacific, Middle East and North Africa, and South Asia.

CHAPTER 2

Understanding Terrorism and Counterterrorism

INTRODUCTION TO COUNTER-TERRORISM

This chapter will focus on the act of terrorism itself and reveal political motivations of terrorism. The purpose of this chapter is to offer the reader a deeper understanding of the kinds of terrorism and their motivation. Before any significant discussion of terrorism can occur, the definition of terrorism and the controversy of this definition must be discussed. This effort is more than just an academic exercise since it is this definition that prompts the term's use in a variety of media. The term "terrorism" is then revealed as politically motivated violence. How this motivation gains supporters and momentum is then uncovered.

© roibu/Shutterstock.com

Belgian soldiers on patrol due to a raised terror threat level.

LEARNING OUTCOMES

1. Comprehend the controversy of defining terrorism
2. Identify the major motivations for political violence
3. Discuss the role of an authoritarian government to motivate terrorism

KEY TERMS

Analyzing intelligence
Asymmetric warfare
Authoritarian
Coercion
Collecting intelligence
Counterinsurgency

Disseminating intelligence
Ideational political violence
Individual political violence
Institutional political
  violence
Intimidation

Political violence
Propaganda
Revolution
Violence

DEFINITION OF TERRORISM

The process of defining terrorism is an important step in identifying what is and, more importantly, what is not terrorism. The FBI and Department of Justice distinguish between "international terrorism" and "domestic terrorism." This distinction assists national security agencies in **collecting**, **analyzing**, and **disseminating intelligence** within the intelligence community. International terrorism is defined as having three characteristics:

1. Involve violent acts or acts dangerous to human life that violate federal or state law;

2. Appear to be intended (i) to intimidate or coerce a civilian population; (ii) to influence the policy of a government by intimidation or coercion; or (iii) to affect the conduct of a government by mass destruction, assassination, or kidnapping; and

3. Occur primarily outside the territorial jurisdiction of the United States, or transcend national boundaries in terms of the means by which they are accomplished, the persons they appear intended to intimidate or coerce, or the locale in which their perpetrators operate or seek asylum.*

In comparison, domestic terrorism replaces the third characteristic with, "occur primarily within the territorial jurisdiction of the United States." Although the distinction is simple to identify theoretically, in practice the distinction is much more difficult to make. The law also defines federal crime terrorism. The two parts of this definition include:

1. Is calculated to influence or affect the conduct of government by intimidation or coercion, or to retaliate against government conduct and

2. Is a violation of one of several listed statutes, including § 930(c) (relating to killing or attempted killing during an attack on a federal facility with a dangerous weapon) and § 1114 (relating to killing or attempted killing of officers and employees of the United States).

---

* (Definitions of Terrorism in the U.S. Code 18 U.S.C. § 2331 defines "international terrorism" and "domestic terrorism" for purposes of Chapter 113B of theCode, entitled "Terrorism")

The definitions bring to light that terrorism is an act of **violence** that is aimed to hurt or kill people and it has a purpose of **intimidation** or **coercion**. What these definitions lack is important. First, an act of terrorism is not required to hurt anyone, that is, the threat of bodily harm is enough to meet the requirements under the above statutes. Second, the terrorist or terrorists need not be part of a larger organization. Unlike gang definitions, which include an organized group of criminals, terrorists do not need to be part of an organization. Third, the purpose of the act is broad as long as that act is related to impacting the government in some way. The impact on the government can be both direct and indirect.

INTRODUCTION TO POLITICAL VIOLENCE

Although legal definitions may differ in the application of the term terrorism, the motivation for terrorism is political in nature. It is a form of **asymmetric warfare** that is the natural choice of a significantly weaker powers to a much greater, generally a government, power. Regardless of whether it is considered freedom fighting, which has a positive connotation, or terrorism, all violence against a population to further some political cause is political violence. Thus, regardless of perspective on the cause, all such acts are political violence. **Political violence** is a violence that is outside of state control and that is politically motivated. It is hostile or aggressive acts motivated by a desire to affect change in the government. **Revolution**, a population's attempt to free themselves from an oppressive force or a perceived oppressive force, is a form of political violence. Political violence can fall into three motivational categories:

- **Institutional** political violence accentuates the repercussions of existing organizations and the associated trends that give rise to political violence. This can include oppression of certain peoples by law, rules, or regulations, all of which limit the people's ability to make appropriate changes in the government in a positive manner. This can also occur when an institution restricts access to jobs, thereby limiting access to basic human needs such as shelter, food, water, or clothing. The consequences of imposing restrictive rules or constraining certain people or groups often culminates in a revolution, or the use of terrorism to combat the inequality. An example of this public push back against an establishment can be seen in Tunisia, Africa, starting in 2010, in what would come to be called the Arab Spring. What started out in Tunisia as peaceful protests and demonstrations, rapidly gained momentum, and spread across the majority of North Africa and into the Middle East. Civilians were influenced by public discontent with local government, human rights violations, economic decline, disparate income levels, a large number of unemployed citizens, and extreme poverty, to resort to revolution to alter the course of the government's decisions that were negatively impacting the lives of the people living under their rule. The government responded to protesters with violence to try and maintain control, and the protesters responded in kind. The leaders of several countries involved either fled their respective countries, resigned their posts, or struck deals to avoid prosecution with newly elected leaders, thus making room for new leaders, laws, and policies in favor of the people they govern.

• **Ideational** political violence is defined as the ideas or beliefs that promote the use of violence. Extreme patriotism, loyalty to one's country, strong advocacy efforts for that country and the desire to see the country overcome oppression or hardship is a major motivator for many citizens in a nation. This concept is often referred to as **nationalism**, and the ideology behind it inspires its citizens to act in whatever means necessary to achieve those goals. In many countries, opposing political parties perceived as the "underdogs" have been known to resort to violence when more peaceful efforts fail to help them achieve their goals in a larger political realm, leaving them with few options except for violence. Perhaps the most commonly recognized, and dangerous, illustration of ideational violence though is religious fundamentalism. **Religious fundamentalism** refers to the belief or beliefs of an individual or group of individuals in the absolute power or authority of a sacred religious text, the teachings of a spiritual leader, a prophet, or God. Religious ideologies can be particularly lethal in the political arena because a person's religion or belief system is such an integral and unwavering part of what makes that person who they are, they are therefore more likely to engage in activities that further their beliefs or protect them from perceived threats. An example of nationalism and religious fundamentalism as a form of ideational political violence can be illustrated by the civil unrest in Iraq beginning with the fall of Saddam Hussein's governmental control in 2003. Hussein seized Presidential power and controlled Iraq from 1979 to 2003 as a Sunni Muslim, one of the two traditional sects of Islam. Eighty to ninety percentages of Muslims worldwide self-identify as Sunni Muslims, leaving 10–20% to self-identify as Shi'a Muslims. In Iraq, however, the distribution is estimated at 32–37% Sunni, and 60–65% Shi'a. After Hussein's execution in 2006, the Shi'a Muslims wanted to regain control of the region. The Shi'a formed small groups and began to launch small-scale attacks on the government. These groups were engaging in **asymmetric warfare**, where the groups' relative military power differs largely from their opponent. This is typically seen between formed, professional armies and insurgents or resistance movements. ISIS (Islamic State of Iraq and Syria) is an example of this type of insurgency and was born of the conflict between Sunni and Shi'a Muslims. The members of groups such as ISIS are motivated by their perceived or real oppression to use whatever means necessary to protect themselves, their people, and their beliefs. These groups typically resort to violence when all other methods fail them, as a way to make their voices heard.

An arms instructor leads a military drill, circa 1999, Baghdad, Iraq.

- **Individual** political violence is defined as a type of violence that occurs when an individual believes that their political or government system will not respond to their demands. The violence occurs as a means of achieving a goal. An example of individual political violence is Ted Kaczynski, otherwise known as the "Unabomber." Considered odd but a child prodigy from a young age, Kaczynski was a highly educated, articulate man who either mailed or hand delivered 16 homemade bombs to individuals at universities and airlines from 1978 to 1995, killing three people and injuring 23 others. Kaczynski was motivated by his belief that the industrial–technological system was irrevocably changing the behavior of the people using it, and called for a "revolution against technology." He called this "the disruption of power process." Kaczynski wrote that he was unsettled by how the "industrial system has robbed contemporary humans of their autonomy, diminished their rapport with nature, and forced them to behave in ways that are increasingly remote from the natural pattern of human behavior." Kaczynski sent or delivered bombs as a means of expressing his views and opinions that he felt were not going to be heard using any other method of communication outside of violence. After 18 years of investigations, the Federal Bureau of Investigations arrested Kaczynski after his "manifesto," also called "*Industrial Society and Its Future*," ***and*** was published in the New York Times and the Washington Post, tipping Kaczynski's brother off to the Unabomber's identity. Ted Kaczynski was later diagnosed with schizophrenia and avoided capital punishment because of this diagnosis. He is currently serving eight consecutive life terms at a Super Maximum Security facility in Florence, Colorado.

The aforementioned motivations should be used to assist in defining the motivation for the group, but real life is not so black and white. Political violence generally begins at the "grassroots" level. Individuals inspire and grow some cause, thus, counterterrorism must accept that motivations change and adapt. A group may change the focus of their cause from one type of motivation into another or it may embody more than one. Therefore, categorizing political motivations should be done to help the analyst but not be part of the analysis.

In addition to motivation, analysts can use the approach of the terrorists to gain insight on their method to inspire more support and advance their cause.

PERSUASION: IDEOLOGY AND RELIGION, ENTICE PEOPLE TO SUPPORT ONE SIDE

This method to advance a cause relies on culture, often through religion, and attaches a cause to a shared belief system or principle. Because this method is often intertwined with culture and religion, it can be difficult to persuade followers otherwise. **Propaganda**, efforts to change the hearts and minds of a population, can be used but the execution of the tactic must be done carefully as not to arouse suspicion. The tactic of influencing the opinions of a population is commonly known as Psychological Operations, or PSYOPs. The process of developing a plan to change the perspective of a population is to:

1. identify the terrorist belief system
2. identify the aspects of the culture that allows the terrorist argument to propagate
3. identify cultural principles that would undermine the terrorist argument
4. identify a method, generally through an individual or group that the population trusts and who seeks political power, to insert a contrary argument that will be accepted by the population
5. make contact and form an alliance with the individual or group that would insert the propaganda
6. ensure the insertion propaganda is shared and that the trusted parties continue to keep their alliance with your cause
7. continue to support the new political system and further marginalize the terrorism argument

COERCION: THE USE OF INTIMIDATION TO GAIN SUPPORT

In contrast to persuasion, coercion relies on the threat of force to further their cause. This tactic is similar to those used by gangs to intimidate community members into turning a blind eye to crimes. Meanwhile, the gang or terrorist group grows by exploiting economic or social conditions. High unemployment or underemployment rates can cause individuals to join a prosperous gang or terrorist group. In addition, individuals seeking a greater cause or family cohesion may join the group. Community members, including those who disapprove of the groups' activities, may distrust law enforcement or the counterterrorism authorities. Gaining the trust of the community is paramount when coercion is used to further a counterinsurgency effort. To accomplish this, humanitarian relief and economic inducements, such as subsidizing local businesses to encourage job growth, can be appropriate methods.

REACTION TO ABUSES: REACTION BY PEOPLE WHEN GOVERNMENT EXCEEDS LOCAL NORMS IN USE OF FORCE

When **authoritarian** governments inflict harm on a population, an antigovernment reaction (possibly terrorism) should be expected unless that government's repressive force is so great that no reaction can be accomplished successfully. Optimally, governments should meet the needs of the people, but if history is any guide, that perspective is rather optimistic. In the Algerian fight for independence from the French, it was the torture techniques that were used by the French that is cited as the motivating for the population to support the terrorist group's cause. The use of torture in obtaining credible intelligence is highly controversial, but it should be noted that counterinsurgency (COIN) operations can be severely hampered if the word of the inappropriate use of torture is made public. Terrorist groups may use torture reports to gain support for their cause. In addition, terrorists may exaggerate or fabricate a foreign government's counterterrorism tactics to garner support.

The aforementioned approaches are three of the most popular insurgency tactics, but many more exist. Terrorist groups may exaggerate the role of foreign support in the form of money or weapons. COIN operations must use accurate intelligence to determine how the terrorist group is garnering support. Although most consider terrorists to be rational, in the sense that they can weigh costs and benefits, it is also possible that some groups operate because they are driven by the desire to fight. Terrorists may be a result of a culture of violence and are thus motivated by the violence alone. It can be argued that this is not terrorism, but instead a criminal act.

Traditional wars are those in which each nation has a formal military and each side attempts to win battles until one must admit defeat due to a lack of resources (money, personnel, equipment, ammunition, etc.). On September 10, 2001 our military was most prepared for such a battle. Structure, culture, and training were designed to prepare the men and women of the military to combat another nation who also had a military. September 11, 2001 was the first of many days in which the military had to change how it fights wars. For many years after 2001, the military continued to use cold war-based strategies. These strategies are what it knew best and those operations were more easily devised and deployed. As the years wore on, strategies needed to change to make our military more effective against a different

September 11, 2001

kind of combatant. Unlike traditional combatants, terrorists will hide behind school children and find shelter in hospitals and places of worship. In addition, how terrorists use the media and disseminate their propaganda is challenging to overcome.

In 2007, the U.S. Army published the new **Counterinsurgency** Field Manual and it marked a new beginning for the operations that should be done in conflicts involving terrorist cells. Unlike traditional military operations, the manual encouraged making connections with the community and fostering trust between the host nation and COIN operations. In essence, the manual makes it clear that winning a war against terrorists means winning the hearts and minds of the people of that nation. Thus, combating terrorism means combating the ideology that inspires terrorism.

GLOSSARY

Analyzing intelligence—The process of taking known information about potential situations and categorizing by importance and probability of the actions happening.

Asymmetric warfare—Opposing groups have unequal military forces. Weaker opponent uses unconventional tactics as terrorism to exploit vulnerabilities.

Authoritarian—A government characterized by absolute obedience to authority.

Coercion—The practice of persuading someone through force or threats.

Collecting intelligence—Process of gathering information then to analyze for intelligence.

Counterinsurgency—Military or political action taken against the activities of guerrillas or revolutionaries.

Disseminating intelligence—Process of delivering the product to the consumer.

Ideational political violence—Political violence is defined as the ideas or beliefs that promote the use of violence.

Individual political violence—Defined as a type of violence that occurs when an individual believes that their political or government system will not respond to their demands.

Institutional political violence—Accentuates the repercussions of existing organizations and the associated trends that give rise to political violence.

Intimidation—The act of intimidating someone.

Political violence—Violence that is outside of state control and that is politically motivated. Hostile or aggressive acts motivated by a desire to affect change in the government.

Propaganda—Information, usually biased, that promotes a certain thought or view.

Revolution—Forcible overthrow of a government or social order.

Violence—Behavior involving physical force with the intent to harm, damage, or kill.

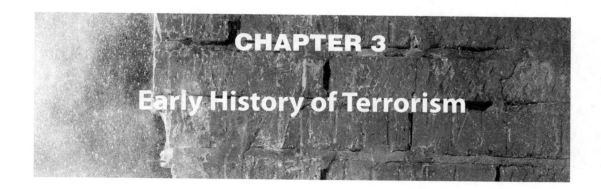

CHAPTER 3
Early History of Terrorism

INTRODUCTION

© ChameleonsEye/Shutterstock.com

The conception of terrorism has changed considerably through history. In recent history the connotation, quite obviously, is one of a **nefarious** counterculture bent on causing harm to innocent civilians in support of an evil cause. It's difficult to appreciate a time when terrorism represented celebrated acts of justice against an unjust government. This chapter will review some major events in the history of

An Egyptian watchtower, upgraded with higher security measures.

terrorism. Particular attention will be paid toward the changing role of terrorism and the motivations of terrorism.

LEARNING OUTCOMES

1. Comprehend the change in the connotation of terrorism
2. Identify the use of terrorism to gain independence from colonial rule
3. Identify the major components of the Atlantic Charter and the role of it in inspiring a fight for independence
4. Evaluate how a terrorist and freedom fighter can be the same group

KEY TERMS

Akritas Plan
Atlantic Charter
Balfour Declaration
Guerrilla
Intercommunal

Jihad
Narodnaya Volya
Nefarious
Red Scare
Regime de la Terreur

Superfluous
Superpower
Zurich Agreement

Narodnaya Volya

The first known example of terrorism occurred during the days of the Russian Empire (1721–1917). That terrorist group, considered the first terrorist group, was Narodnaya Volya. In 1878, a group known as Narodnaya Volya, or "The People's Will," came about in Russia. It was a small group of Russian constitutionalists that challenged the tsar's rule. The group used daring and dramatic acts of violence to attract attention to itself and their cause. The terrorist group sought democratic and social reforms. More specifically, they called for a creation of a constitution, universal suffrage to citizens, freedom of expression, and permission to transfer of land and factories to peasants and laborers who worked in them (*Hoffman, 1998*).

They used "propaganda by deed," which meant the selective targeting of specific individuals whom the group thought of as the symbol of the autocratic, oppressive state. Narodnaya Volya believed that "not one drop of **superfluous** blood" should be shed in pursuit of their purpose, however noble or utilitarian they might be, and they harbored regrets about taking the life of a fellow human being (*Hoffman, 1998*). After the group assassinated Tsar Alexander II in 1881, the full weight of the government efforts to eradicate them lead to their demise. In public displays, the Russians executed the last member in 1883.

Although the group was unsuccessful in overthrowing the Russian government, they did succeed in starting a tide against the Russian Empire that eventually did fail due to following campaigns. The People's Will highlights that terrorist groups need not be "evil." In France, terrorism was viewed far more positively.

The Regime de la Terreur

The *regime de la terreur* was adopted in 1793 during the French Revolution. They meant to establish order during a time of chaos and upheaval following the uprisings of 1789. The *regime de la terreur* was a system of governance that was designed to strengthen the new government's power by subduing counterrevolutionaries, subversives, and all other dissidents, whom the new regime considered as "enemies of the people." Thus, the *regime de la terreur* was an instrument that opposed those that impeded the revolution. Within the government, the court was given wide powers to arrest and judge, which publicly put to death all persons who committed treason, thus enforcing a powerful message to all who might oppose the regime.

The storming of the Bastille, 1789.

The *regime de la terreur* was neither random nor indiscriminate as terrorism is portrayed today; it was organized, deliberate, and systematic. Its goal was to create a better society in place of a corrupt system. The regime came to an end when it was announced that a new list of traitors had come about, in fear that their names might be on it, extremists joined forces to tear down the regime. After this, terrorism became a term associated with abuse of office and power, and was seen as a criminal act (*Hoffman, 1998*).

ASSASSINATION OF U.S. PRESIDENT WILLIAM MCKINLEY

The assassination of U.S. President William McKinley in 1901, by a young Hungarian refugee, Leon Czolgosz, led to quick action by congress and marked a change in the connotation of the word "terrorism." As discussed, terrorism had a positive connotation that represented a method that citizens could oppose an unjust government. Congress enacted legislation barring known anarchists or anyone "who disbelieves in or is opposed to all organized government" from entering the United States, causing the "**Red Scare.**" Feelings against anarchists' and alien citizens created the movement's emphasis on individual action or operations carried out by small cells of like-minded radicals, made detection and prevention by the police particularly difficult, thus further heightening public fears (*Hoffman, 1998*).

President Woodrow Wilson in 1916.

It was at this time that the term "terrorist" changed from someone that could be a neighbor or friend to one that identified an outsider that purposed to harm. Terrorism then changes from a term reflecting the desire of a small group of individuals to a larger population. The events that precipitated this change can first be identified in 1918 with Woodrow Wilson's Fourteen Points. In this speech to the U.S. Congress, Wilson outlines the 14 actions to promote peace after World War I. The 14 points are listed here:

I. Open covenants of peace, openly arrived at, after which there shall be no private international understandings of any kind but diplomacy shall proceed always frankly and in the public view.

II. Absolute freedom of navigation upon the seas, outside territorial waters, alike in peace and in war, except as the seas may be closed in whole or in part by international action for the enforcement of international covenants.

III. The removal, so far as possible, of all economic barriers and the establishment of an equality of trade conditions among all the nations consenting to the peace and associating themselves for its maintenance.

IV. Adequate guarantees given and taken that national armaments will be reduced to the lowest point consistent with domestic safety.

V. A free, open-minded, and absolutely impartial adjustment of all colonial claims, based upon a strict observance of the principle that in determining all such questions of sovereignty the interests of the populations concerned must have equal weight with the equitable claims of the government whose title is to be determined.

VI. The evacuation of all Russian territory and such a settlement of all questions affecting Russia as will secure the best and freest cooperation of the other nations of the world in obtaining for her an unhampered and unembarrassed opportunity for the independent determination of her own political development and national policy and assure her of a sincere welcome into the society of free nations under institutions of her own choosing; and, more than a welcome, assistance also of every kind that she may need and may herself desire. The treatment accorded Russia by her sister nations in the months to come will be the acid test of their good will, of their comprehension of her needs as distinguished from their own interests, and of their intelligent and unselfish sympathy.

VII. Belgium, the whole world will agree, must be evacuated and restored, without any attempt to limit the sovereignty which she enjoys in common with all other free nations. No other single act will serve as this will serve to restore confidence among the nations in the laws which they have themselves set and determined for the government of their relations with one another. Without this healing act, the whole structure and validity of international law is forever impaired.

VIII. All French territory should be freed and the invaded portions restored, and the wrong done to France by Prussia in 1871 in the matter of Alsace-Lorraine, which has unsettled the peace of the world for nearly 50 years, should be righted, in order that peace may once more be made secure in the interest of all.

IX. A readjustment of the frontiers of Italy should be effected along clearly recognizable lines of nationality.

X. The peoples of Austria-Hungary, whose place among the nations we wish to see safeguarded and assured, should be accorded the freest opportunity to autonomous development.

XI. Rumania, Serbia, and Montenegro should be evacuated; occupied territories restored; Serbia accorded free and secure access to the sea; and the relations of the several Balkan states to one another determined by friendly counsel along historically established lines of allegiance and nationality; and international guarantees of the political and economic independence and territorial integrity of the several Balkan states should be entered into.

XII. The Turkish portion of the present Ottoman Empire should be assured a secure sovereignty, but the other nationalities which are now under Turkish rule should be assured an undoubted security of life and an absolutely unmolested opportunity of autonomous development, and the Dardanelles should be permanently opened as a free passage to the ships and commerce of all nations under international guarantees.

XIII. An independent Polish state should be erected which should include the territories inhabited by indisputably Polish populations, which should be assured a free and secure access to the sea, and whose political and economic independence and territorial integrity should be guaranteed by international covenant.

XIV. A general association of nations must be formed under specific covenants for the purpose of affording mutual guarantees of political independence and territorial integrity to great and small states alike.

Ironically, the Fourteen Points designed to promote peace elucidated the feelings among civilizations around the world that sought to rid themselves of colonial rule. The reaction to Wilson's Fourteen Points was highly critical and some even claimed that it added nothing toward a solution. During World War I, it was used as propaganda to encourage the troops of the Central Powers to surrender in hopes of a promising outcome.

Although Wilson's Fourteen Points do not call for terrorism of any kind and, in fact, is an attempt to search for peace. It does, however, outline and publicize a motivation for the terrorism that followed World War II. To see the influence of the concepts first raised in the Fourteen Points,

© Sergey Goryachev/Shutterstock.com

President Franklin Roosevelt and British Prime Minister Winston Churchill.

it is important to note when the major obstacle to terrorism against a superpower was over-come. The major obstacle was the impression that a superpower, specifically the British government, could not be defeated.

A major turning point for the proliferation of terrorism occurred during World War II when the Japanese were able to secure control of Singapore in 1942. Prior to this point in history, the British military was considered undefeatable. This marks a major shift in the minds of those throughout the world—the "white man could be defeated." Following Singapore, the British also lost control of Philippines, Burma, Indonesia, and Hong Kong to the Japanese. These defeats further gave the world population the idea that a superpower can be beaten through strategic planning and a greater will. Although the United States was able to eventually defeat the Japanese, the impression that the giant can be defeated continues today (*Hoffman, 1998*).

In conjunction with the defeat of the British in Singapore, the Philippines, Burma Indonesia, and Hong Kong, the impression that a civilization should have rights to their own destiny continued to prosper. In August of 1941, the Atlantic Charter was signed by Winston Churchill and Franklin Roosevelt. The Atlantic Charter outlined actions very similar to that of Wilson's Fourteen Points:

AUGUST 14, 1941

The President of the United States of America and the Prime Minister, Mr. Churchill, representing His Majesty's Government in the United Kingdom, being met together, deem it right to make known certain common principles in the national policies of their respective countries on which they base their hopes for a better future for the world.

First, their countries seek no aggrandizement, territorial or other;

Second, they desire to see no territorial changes that do not accord with the freely expressed wishes of the peoples concerned;

Third, they respect the right of all peoples to choose the form of government under which they will live; and they wish to see sovereign rights and self government restored to those who have been forcibly deprived of them;

Fourth, they will endeavor, with due respect for their existing obligations, to further the enjoyment by all States, great or small, victor or vanquished, of access, on equal terms, to the trade and to the raw materials of the world which are needed for their economic prosperity;

Fifth, they desire to bring about the fullest collaboration between all nations in the economic field with the object of securing, for all, improved labor standards, economic advancement and social security;

Sixth, after the final destruction of the Nazi tyranny, they hope to see established a peace which will afford to all nations the means of dwelling in safety within their own boundaries, and which will afford assurance that all the men in all lands may live out their lives in freedom from fear and want;

Seventh, such a peace should enable all men to traverse the high seas and oceans without hindrance;

Eighth, they believe that all of the nations of the world, for realistic as well as spiritual reasons must come to the abandonment of the use of force. Since no future peace can be maintained if land, sea or air armaments continue to be employed by nations which threaten, or may threaten, aggression outside of their frontiers, they believe, pending the establishment of a wider and permanent system of general security, that the disarmament of such nations is essential. They will likewise aid and encourage all other practicable measure which will lighten for peace-loving peoples the crushing burden of armaments.

Franklin D. Roosevelt
Winston S. Churchill

- **Atlantic Charter** (http://avalon.law.yale.edu/wwii/atlantic.asp):

Following the signing of the Atlantic Charter, the people of colonized areas looked forward to governmental freedom, but the owning nations did not abide by the Atlantic Charter's concepts. Two such cases are the process of independence of Algeria from France and Cyprus from the British.

INDEPENDENCE OF ALGERIA

During the 1950s, there was a struggle in Algeria against France and its settlers for independence, which caused hatred in both countries toward the other. The French conquest occurred in the 1830s and in 1848; Algeria was annexed into three French departments. Traditional land ownership was dismantled, and French colonizers were allowed to buy or confiscate it. In 1954, racial, economic, cultural, and political lines polarized Algeria, and the difference between the French Algerians and the Algerians created violence. The Algerian War started on November 1, 1954, and lasted until 1962, when Algeria gained independence (*Hoffman, 1998*).

INDEPENDENCE OF CYPRUS

On August 16, 1960, Cyprus gained its independence from the United Kingdom, after a long anti-British campaign by a Greek **guerrilla** group that desired a political union with Greece, known as the Greek Cypriot. After Cyprus gained its independence, the **Zurich Agreement** was created; it was designed to establish cooperation between the Greek Cypriot and the Turkish Cypriot, since the country was torn between wanting a political union with Greece and wanting a political union with Turkey, however the agreement did not succeed and both sides continued violence. In 1963, President Makarios, the president of Cyprus, created a series of constitutional amendments that the Turkish Cypriots opposed, and created widespread **intercommunal** fighting in December 1963. The **Akritas plan** was then put into motion that put an end to the Turkish Cypriot participation in the government. Due to the forced withdrawal of the Turkish Cypriots, the Cyprus government was no longer functional or legal. United Nation Peacekeepers were deployed to Cyprus in 1964, to prevent fighting, and to maintain law and order; they also effectively recognized the Greek Cypriots as government. The President was then overthrown by the 1974 Cypriot coup d'etat, which lead to the Turkish invasion in July of 1974. Turkey took control of 38% of the island. After this, the southern part of Cyprus was internationally recognized as the government of Cyprus, and the northern part was recognized as the government of northern Cyprus.

In 1983, the northern government of Cyprus, which was under control by Turkish Cypriots declared itself as the Turkish Republic of Northern Cyprus, which was only recognized by Turkey. The United Nation's Peacekeeping forces still maintain a buffer zone between the two sides, and except for occasional demonstrations, there is now little violence. In 2003, the buffer zone was partly opened and both sides could go about freely, in 2004, Cyprus joined the European Union and in 2014, leaders of the Greek Cypriots and Turkish Cypriots produced an unprecedented joint declaration for a negotiated settlement (*Hoffman, 1998*).

PALESTINIAN–ISRAELI CONFLICT

The Palestinian–Israeli conflict has been occurring for much longer than most people realize, and it is a tale of conflict between two cultures. The Arab people descended from Nomads and after the seventh century, they united under the leadership of Mohammed. The Jewish people lived throughout the area and Europe, and were discriminated against in Eastern Europe and Russia. The Israelis believe that 6000 years ago God directed Abraham to the Promised Land where Israel is now located; "....and to thy seed after thee, the land wherein thou art a stranger, and the land of Canaan, for an everlasting possession," Genesis 17:8. By the nineteenth century, however, the Jewish people no longer wanted to return to the Promised Land.

In the 1890s, the **Zionist movement** began, Theodor Herzl wrote *The Jewish State* in 1896 and spoke about a Jewish state that freed the Jewish people from persecution. He influenced the British and a settlement was nearly made in British East Africa however, the Russian Zionist Jews refused the proposal because it was not the Promised Land which was now occupied by Arab people and was known as Palestine. When Herzl died, Chaim Weizmann took over, and his scientific achievements gave his perspective on Zionism more notice. His efforts with the British to prevent Turkish rule resulted in the **Balfour Declaration**:

Foreign Office
November 2nd, 1917

Dear Lord Rothschild,

I have much pleasure in conveying to you, on behalf of His Majesty's Government, the following declaration of sympathy with Jewish Zionist aspirations which has been submitted to, and approved by, the Cabinet.

"His Majesty's Government view with favour the establishment in Palestine of a national home for the Jewish people, and will use their best endeavours to facilitate the achievement of this object, it being clearly understood that nothing shall be done which may prejudice the civil and religious rights of existing non-Jewish communities in Palestine, or the rights and political status enjoyed by Jews in any other country."

I should be grateful if you would bring this declaration to the knowledge of the Zionist Federation.

Yours sincerely,
Arthur James Balfour
(http://avalon.law.yale.edu/20th_century/balfour.asp)

The Balfour Declaration became a cornerstone for the argument for a state of Israel. When interpreted, the Arabs thought it meant that the Jewish people should live within the Arab state of Palestine, but the Jewish people thought the reverse. The British then promised the Arabs an independent kingdom of their own if they revolted against the Ottoman Turks.

By 1925, immigration had become a major concern, and with open borders, Jewish people streamed in. The Sephardic Jews that already lived in the area years before and spoke Arabic were viewed with contempt by the new Ashkenazic Jews, who viewed themselves as Europeans and refused to learn Arabic. The two groups of Jewish people conflicted, each having their own claim to the area, and soon incidents began to occur. One such incident involved was at the Wailing Wall. The Wailing Wall, or Western Wall, is considered one of the holiest places where Jews are allowed to pray. It is also considered Holy by the Muslims, as it is cited as the place where the Prophet Mohammad tied his horse Buraq, before ascending the Heaven. Several benches for the weak and ill were removed after the Palestinians protested because nobody was allowed to construct anything in range of the wall. Screens separating the men and women were also removed with force, after a complaint was issued. The Arabs then tried to distract Jewish worshippers, and the Jewish communities claimed that this was denial of religious freedoms.

ISRAEL GETS INDEPENDENCE

Following the White Paper in 1939, a British policy paper penned by Neville Chamberlain in response to the 1936–1939 Arab Revolt, limited the Jews from entering into Palestine, and revolts against the British ensued, lead primarily by the terrorist group, Irgun. During this time, the British were also heavily fighting in World War II, thus, Irgun suspended their attacks to allow the British to focus on the War. Following the War, Irgun continued their campaign for an independent Jewish state. Irgun's leader, Begin, knew that the British were hampered by their own ideology that repression was not permitted. Therefore, Irgun merely needed to not lose the fight and wait for the British people to become tired of fighting. The goal was to impact their opponents on a psychological level, not only physical. The group severely undermined the British, not by winning but simply to continue to "not lose." Terrorist events, varying in success pushed the British people further into war fatigue. Even "unsuccessful" attacks still managed to put a dent in the prestige of the British military.

The breaking point occurred after the King David Hotel bombing (*Hoffman, 1998*) in 1946. The King David Hotel had British soldiers in the basement of the building. Prior to the bombing, the hotel was notified of the bomb's existence. Staff and police quickly evacuated the building, but not the soldiers in the basement. Because of this, the deaths of the soldiers were being printed on the front page of the newspaper. With that, the British people had endured enough, and shortly after, the British quickly took steps to create the Jewish state of Israel. In 1949, Israel was given statehood from Palestine, but statehood was given hastily, as the British were anxious to put an end to the terrorism.

THE UNITED STATES AND THE SOVIET UNION

In order to make a Jewish state, Palestinians living in the area soon to be Israel were displaced. These Palestinians expected their departure to be temporary so they populated refugee camps under the expectation that the Arab army would regain control of the land known as Israel. They remained in refugee camps in Syria, Lebanon, Egypt, and Jordan and identified themselves as displaced citizens. The Arab Army did not want to combat the Israelis again, and the refugees continued to wait and become frustrated. Teams of individuals from the camps created commando units and attacked Israeli forces who were across the border. Leaving their camps deep in the night, the commandos began a long history of frequent attacks on Israeli forces.

As the actions of the Palestinian commandos gained notice, the Egyptian President, Nasser, exploited the situation in an effort to gain support to become the leader of the Arab states. Egypt trained and gave weapons to the commandos in an effort to put more pressure on the Israelis. Then, in February of 1953, the USSR broke off relations with Israel and begins a pro-Arab middle eastern policy, they send weapons in support of the Arabs. In an effort to close the supply lines to the Israelis, Nasser denied Israeli ships by blocking the Straits of Tiran. This route was the primary path by which the Israelis received oil, thus, this was a major constriction to the Israelis.

Several conflicts were instrumental to the current state of the Israeli–Palestinian conflict. The preemptive strike against Arab forces on June 6, 1967, resulted in a 6-day conflict. This event is known as the 6-Day War. The conflict resulted in the Israelis successfully capturing

Jerusalem—the heart of the "Promised Land." Another important conflict is the October 1973 war. This conflict's unintended impact was establishing the assumption that the United States was aligned with Israel, as the USSR supported Egypt. The assumption later grew into an expectation and today this is considered to be in some way unofficial policy. Yet, during the October 1973 War, the U.S. State Department was startled to hear that the U.S.–Israeli relationship was assumed to be so codified in the minds of leaders around the world. With U.S. aid, Syria and Egypt acknowledged the military superiority of Israel. The continued expectation that the United States would support Israel's policies and actions has made the United States a target for groups and countries that oppose the Israeli stance on a variety of issues.

REFUGEES

In the process of making a new Jewish state in Palestine, now known as Israel, some 950,000 Arab-Palestinians became refugees. These Palestinian refugees stayed in camps and waited to go back to what is now Israel. This anxious waiting led to more hostility and terrorist events against Israel. In 2010, 7.1 million refugees lived as a displaced population and this population outnumbered the Israeli population (http://www.irinnews.org/report/89571/middle-east-palestinian-refugee-numbers-whereabouts).

GLOSSARY

Akritas Plan—A plan that put an end to the Turkish Cypriot participation in the Cyprus government.

Atlantic Charter—Policy statement issued in August 14, 1941, that defined the Allied goals for the postwar world.

Balfour Declaration—A letter from the United Kingdom to Baron Rothschild for transmission to the Zionist Federation of Great Britain and Ireland.

Guerrilla—Small independent group taking part in irregular fighting.

Intercommunal—Shared in common with a group of people.

Jihad—Islamic term referring to a religious duty of Muslims. A noun meaning "struggle" or "resisting."

Narodnaya Volya (aka Peoples' Will)—Terrorist group that operated during the Russian Empire.

Nefarious—Wicked or criminal.

Red Scare—Promotion of fear and the potential rise of Communism.

Regime de la Terreur (aka The Terror)—the revolutionary mechanism that acted against those that opposed the revolution.

Superfluous—Unnecessary and excessive.

Superpower—A very powerful and influential nation.

Zurich Agreement—An agreement designed to create cooperation between the Greek Cypriot and the Turkish Cypriot in Cyprus.

CHAPTER 4

Role of Law Enforcement and Intelligence in Combating Terrorism

INTRODUCTION

This chapter will review the role of law enforcement and intelligence. Although their roles may seem intertwined to the public, the manner by which they operate and their purposes are very different. Policing is law enforcement, but law enforcement is not policing. Policing eludes to a relationship with the community; this relationship is built over time with interaction

NYPD emergency services.

between the police and the public. Law enforcement agencies such as the Federal Bureau of Investigations (FBI), Drug Enforcement Agency (DEA), and Alcohol, Tobacco, and Firearms (ATF) do not "walk the beat." That said the role of law enforcement is important to the counterterrorism effort as they are more specialized and are equipped better than most police departments. Intelligence is very different in the role it plays in counterterrorism. Intelligence provides valuable information to inform policymakers and agencies. In this chapter, the role of all police and intelligence will be reviewed.

LEARNING OUTCOMES

1. Identify the role of police as a counterterrorism tool
2. Identify the role of intelligence as a counterterrorism tool
3. Describe the role of the policymakers and their relationship with intelligence

KEY TERM

Noise (intelligence)

LAW ENFORCEMENT

Law enforcement agencies in the United States are comprised of three different levels: federal, state, and local agencies. All of these agencies are tasked with the investigation of suspected criminal activity, the referral of investigation results to the judicial branch for trial, and temporarily maintaining custody of suspected criminals pending judicial action. The agencies are also tasked with being both proactive and reactive, by attempting to deter criminal activity and preventing crimes already in progress. Federal law enforcement agencies include the FBI, DEA, and the ATF. All 50 states each have their own law enforcement agencies as well, and most major cities and small towns have their own law enforcement agencies as well, each with varying degrees of capabilities and personnel numbers. The New York Police Department (NYPD) in New York City was created in 1845 and has roughly 34,450 uniformed officers on their roster, with an additional 4,500 auxiliary police officers, 5,000 school safety officers, and 2,300 officers who deal with only traffic enforcement issues.

The NYPD, along with many major law enforcement agencies, now have Counterterrorism Units. These units are comprised of many subunits with wide ranging capabilities and responsibilities. The subunits include but are not limited to: the Technology and Construction Section, which designs and implements large-scale counterterrorism projects; the Training Section, which develops and delivers counterterrorism training to the patrol force and to other law enforcement agencies; the Chemical, Biological, Radiological, Nuclear, and Explosives (CBRNE) Section, which research and test emerging technologies used to detect and combat CBRNE weapons; the Maritime Team, who are responsible for researching and developing systems and programs to increase harbor security; the NYPD SHIELD Unit, which manages the department's public–private security partnership, providing training and information to the private sector; and the Emergency Preparedness and Exercise Section, which work closely with the New York City office of Emergency Management.

In addition to these, the NYPD also has a Joint Terrorism Task Force (JTTC), a partnership with the FBI. After September 11, 2001, the NYPD raised the number of detectives and supervisors involved with the JTTC from 17 to 125, with hope that higher personnel numbers would be better able to help protect the NYC metro area from terrorist attacks. The NYPD JTTC has allowed the NYPD to disperse its own intelligence and analysis at the federal level, and increases communication between law enforcement agencies. The NYPD JTTC has also taken the lead on several high-profile international terrorism cases, like the attack on the U.S.S. Cole, and the U.S. Embassy bombings in Eastern Africa.

The NYPD also has what it called the Lower Manhattan Security Initiative, a networked surveillance project designed to detect threat and perform preoperational terrorist surveillance south of Canal Street in Lower Manhattan. Using a combination of omnipresence of uniformed officers and technology, this program seeks to prevent terrorist attacks in the nation's financial capital by constantly collecting information and intelligence for analysis.

The Terrorism Threat Analysis Group is the part of the NYPD that performs strategic intelligence analysis and passes the information to its respective department in the main Department, the private sector, and the U.S. intelligence community.

Los Angeles, California, also has a strong and diverse counterterrorism program.

The Counter-Terrorism and Special Operations Bureau has several divisions, including the Major Crimes Division, which investigates individuals or group who plan, threaten, finance, aid, abet, attempt, or perform unlawful acts which threaten public safety. This division includes the Criminal Conspiracy Section, Intelligence Investigations Section, Liaison Section, and the Surveillance Section.

The Emergency Services Division serves the city of Los Angeles by preventing or mitigating terrorist or other criminal activities using threat assessments, detection, and deterrence and by responding quickly to criminal incidents. This division houses the Emergency Planning Section, The Emergency Operations Section, the Field and Community Support Section, Hazardous Devices Section, the Bomb Squad Unit, the Hazardous Materials Unit, and the Operations Section.

The Los Angeles Metro Division is made up of five field-based platoons, and all

Los Angeles Police Department's rescue truck.

tasked with different duties. The Operations Platoon handles the administrative and support functions in the field, while two platoons are primarily responsible for suppressing crime. The Special Weapons and Tactics Unit (SWAT) and the K-9 Unit are available as necessary, as are the platoon that responds to emergency situations encompassing hostages or barricaded suspects.

Los Angeles PD also has an Air Support Division. Beginning in 1956, the Air Support Division, or the "Helicopter Unit," was created with just one helicopter as a means of traffic law enforcement. In 1974, the unit boasted 77 sworn personnel and 15 helicopters in its fleet. A NASA study confirmed that Part 1 Property Crimes are reduced when a LAPD Helicopter is overhead. In 2016, the Air Support Division maintains 88 sworn personnel.

MILITARIZATION OF POLICE DEPARTMENTS

In light of recent events on not only a national, but also a global platform, America has seen an increase in the militarization of police. This involves the increase in use of military grade equipment and tactics by law enforcement officers. This includes but is not limited to the use of armored personnel carriers, submachine guns, grenade launchers, sniper rifles, and SWAT teams. Present day, American law enforcement agencies have become "military-esque," in that their uniforms, weapons, vehicles, etc., have become far more militarized, and the gap between what used to be a paramilitary institution and a military institution has closed significantly.

The militarization of police departments changes the mentality and view of law enforcement from both sides. On the law enforcement side, it encourages officers to adopt a "warrior" mentality, fostering the mindset that the people they are supposed to serve are "the enemy." On the civilian side, the militarization of police makes the "us versus them" mentality more clear as the law enforcement officers are perceived to be treating "us" as the enemy. This tenuous relationship shifts the balance of what was once believed to be a "serve and protect" position to a possible abuse of power position, causing unease and discomfort with law enforcement and their perceived role in the day-to-day interactions with civilians.

Because of this general discontent, many departments have changed their hiring processes to include not only the physical and written exams, the oral board interviews, the polygraph testing, and background checks, but also sensitivity training, antibias training, police diversity training, and cultural awareness training for all officers. These workshops and trainings foster stronger relationships between the police and the civilian populations, by encouraging police to view the people they serve as people with families, jobs, and bills, just as they are. It also encourages the civilians to be more trusting of those within the department, and view the officers as people with families, jobs, and bill, just as they are. This hiring and continuing education practice will hopefully lead to stronger, more trusting relationships across the gap of "us versus them."

Community policing is another way of bridging the gap between the police and the communities they serve. Community policing is the system of allocating police officers to particular areas so that they become familiar with the local inhabitants. Under this policing model, law enforcement agencies along with the individuals and organizations in the community they serve work together to develop solutions to problems, garnering increased trust in the police from the civilian side and a sense of partnership, and working collaboratively toward common goals of decreasing crime and increasing the general safety of the public.

Community policing is often used in the de-escalation of situations, as opposed to using force. De-escalation is defined as decreasing the intensity or magnitude of a problem. The Dallas Police Department in Dallas, Texas, is confident that de-escalation techniques work better than force. Dallas Police Chief David Brown reports that "In 2009, the department received 147 excessive force complaints and made 74,000 arrests. Within 3 years, arrests were down to 61,000, and within 5 years excessive force complaints were down to 53. As the number of excessive force complaints and arrests declined, so did the city's murder rate, which reached its lowest point in more than 80 years in 2014, before ticking back upward in 2015." The de-escalation training encourages greater community outreach, emphasis on officers slowing down to try to avoid use of force, stronger communication between officers and civilians, particularly in tense situations, and taking the time to form a strategy before acting in any given situation, and trying to build a rapport with suspects instead of making assumptions about their guilt or innocence and acting rashly.

An important aspect of Homeland Security is the element of Military Force. Surprisingly, many practitioners of Emergency Management fail to recognize the role of the Department of Defense (DOD) in Homeland Security and how their capabilities can be utilized by civil authorities. Often, the DOD is dismissed as an option due to the misperceptions of Posse Comitatus Act (PCA) of 1878 (18 U.S.C. § 1385). This law prohibits the direct active participation of military forces to execute civilian laws unless otherwise authorized by law. Often overlooked is Immediate Response Authority (IRA) granted to military commanders. IRA allows commanders to execute certain resources in response to a request from civil authorities, temporarily employing the resources under their control, to save lives, prevent human suffering, or mitigate great property damage within the United States. Immediate response is situation specific and may or may not be associated with a declared or undeclared disaster, civil emergency, incident, or attack.

This section will provide background information on Posse Comitatus and the various roles and capabilities available from the DOD under the IRA. The goal of this discussion is to ensure that practitioners of Emergency Management garner an understanding of the resources available whether you are a planner or an Incident Commander.

WHAT IS INTELLIGENCE?

As defined by Lowenthal (2015), Intelligence is "the process by which specific types of information important to national security are requested, collected, analyzed, and provided to policymakers; the products of that process; the safeguarding of these processes and this information by counterintelligence activities; and the carrying out of operations as requested by lawful authorities."

Today's intelligence community is made of 17 agencies that work independently and together to create intelligence for the purpose of action and policymaking. The process of creating viable information that can be created into intelligence requires operators and analysts to work together. Operators are tasked with gathering information. This may be done by operators that gather information in performing their job. In this case, intelligence gathering is a secondary mission. On the other hand, intelligence operators may be given a cover for the purpose for gathering information. In this case, intelligence gathering is a primary function. For these individuals, it is vital that they understand how analysis is conducted and can gather information that analysts may need. Gathering all information creates too much **noise** and can impede the analysis process.

Intelligence agencies exist for at least four major reasons:

1. *To avoid strategic surprise*

Intelligence has the foremost goal to keep track of threats, forces, events, and developments that are capable of endangering the nation. This is what is capable of influencing an operation or mission.

2. *To provide long-term expertise*

The average time for a president to be in office is 5 years, secretaries of state and defense serve less than that, and their senior subordinates hold positions even less than that. Thus, the intelligence community is tasked with providing long-term support that goes well before and after political leaders leave their positions. This requires that intelligence reports are not politically influenced or are biased. Keep in mind that these reports can be used years later.

All individuals enter with an extensive background in their field but it is impossible for them to be well versed in every matter they will have to deal with. They have to call upon others whose knowledge on certain issues is greater; much of the expertise on national security resides in the intelligence community.

3. *To support the policy process*

Policymakers have a constant need for tailored, timely intelligence that provides background, context, information, warning, and an assessment of risks, benefits, and likely outcomes. The intelligence community serves the policymaker by providing unbiased assessments.

Although policymakers use intelligence, Intelligence and policy are seen as two separate functions. The government is run by policymakers and intelligence plays a support role.

4. *To maintain the secrecy of information, needs, and methods*

Others (terrorist group, another government, or an individual) keep information from our government, yet our government is in need of certain types of information and we wish to keep these needs secret. Therefore, the intelligence community has to obtain information that we also wish to keep secret. In short, what we know and what we want to know is secret.

The U.S. intelligence community is generally seen as being hierarchical and bureaucratic.

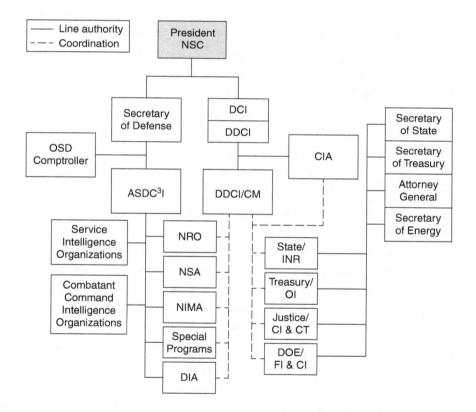

The intelligence community has two broad functional areas:

- Management: Covers requirements, resources, collection, and production.
- Execution: Covers the development of collection systems, the collection and production of intelligence, and the maintenance of the infrastructure support base.

THE INTELLIGENCE PROCESS

Intelligence process refers to the steps or stages in intelligence from policymakers perceiving a need for information to the community's delivery of an analytical intelligence product to them. The seven stages of the intelligence process:

1. Identifying requirements: Defining the policy issues or areas in which the intelligence is expected to make a contribution, as well as deciding which issue has priority over others. This may mean specifying the collection of certain types of intelligence. In addition, some requirements will be better met by specific types of collection.

2. Collection: Produces information not intelligence. Once information is gathered, it must go on to the next step.

3. Processing and exploitation: Before information is decided if it is intelligence it must go to analysts who will determine what is intelligence and what is not, they also may need to decode some of the intelligence.

4. Analysis and production: Analysts then turn the gathered information into reports that respond to the needs of policymakers.

5. Dissemination: The moving of the intelligence from production to consumers. Decisions must be made about how widely the intelligence should be distributed and how urgently it should be passed or flagged for the policymakers' attention.

6. Consumption: How the policymakers consume the information and the degree to which the intelligence is used.

7. Feedback: A dialogue between intelligence consumers and producers should take place after the intelligence has been received, yet this does not occur as often as the intelligence community desires. Policymakers should give some sense of how the intelligence is being used and the requirements are being met as well as make clear any adjustments that should be made to any part of the process.

Without collection, intelligence is little more than guesswork. The United States uses multiple means of collecting intelligence; these means are driven by two factors: the nature of the intelligence being sought and the ability to acquire it in various ways. The means of collecting intelligence is often referred to as "collection disciplines" or INTs. These means include: geospatial intelligence (GEOINT), signals intelligence (SIGINT), human intelligence (HUMINT), open-source intelligence (OSINT), and measurement and signal intelligence (MASINT).

Despite all of the attention that is given on the operational side of intelligence, analysis is the most important part of the process. The analysis provides policymakers with information directly related to issues they face and the decisions they have to make. The ideal intelligence process model includes policymakers giving thought to their main requirements for intelligence and then communicating it to intelligence managers, this rarely happens.

Intelligence can be directed toward addressing current, and possibly short-term, threats or long-term intelligence that develops over the course of years or decades. Intelligence analysts deal with a varying amount of information and certainly of what is truly happening. Analysts must give the best information they can without understating or overstating the intelligence that they procured. Misinformation can impact policy or relations for years to come.

Counterintelligence refers to efforts taken to protect one's own intelligence operations from penetration and disruption by hostile nations or their intelligence services.

There are at least three types of counterintelligence:

- Collection: Gaining information about an opponent's intelligence collection capabilities that may be aimed at one's own country.
- Defensive: Thwarting efforts by hostile intelligence services to penetrate one's service.
- Offensive: Having identified an opponent's efforts against one's own system and trying to manipulate these attacks either by turning the opponents' agents into double agents or by feeding them false information that they report home.

Covert action remains one of the most controversial and misunderstood intelligence topics. These actions are secret but they are undertaken for means to advance policy goals. Proper covert actions are undertaken because policymakers have determined that they are the best way to achieve a desired end. These operations do not, or should not, proceed on the initiative of the intelligence agencies. Policymakers need a third option between doing nothing in a situation which vital interests may be threatened or sending military forces. Thus, the planning process must begin with policymakers justifying the policy, defining the national security interests and goals, and believing that covert action is a viable means as well as the best means for achieving a specific end.

Covert actions encompass many types of activities:

- Propaganda: The old political technique of disseminating information that has been created with a specific political outcome in mind. It can be used to support individuals on the one side and undermine others.
- Political activity: A step above propaganda, enables an intelligence operation to intervene more directly in the political process of the targeted nation.
- Economic: Every leadership worries about its economy because it has the greatest daily effect on the population.

- Sabotage: The deliberate destruction of property or facilities. It can be a straightforward effort to subvert on going activities.

- Coups: The overthrowing of a government.

- Paramilitary operations: The largest, most violent, and most dangerous of covert actions, involving the equipping and training of large armed groups for a direct assault on one's enemies. They do not involve the use of a state's own military personnel in combatant units.

THE ROLE OF THE POLICYMAKER

The ultimate goal of the U.S. policy process is to arrive at a consensus that all parties can support. Intelligence provides a means by which policymakers can become informed and make the best choices. Despite the fact that policymakers rely on the intelligence reports and briefing that are produced, policymakers tend to be divorced from the details of collection unless they involve political sensitivities. Instead policymakers focus on information that enables them to make an informed decision. They like to see intelligence that supports their preferences, but it is the analyst's job to be free of bias. Bias originating in intelligence has clouded some policy and has produced missteps. For example, an informant named "Curveball" provided information that directly leads to the invasion of Iraq in 2003. The intelligence that he provided indicated that Weapons of Mass Destruction (WMDs) were in Iraq and that the government had the will and means to deploy them. After almost a decade, no such WMDs were found. It is widely suspected that the Curveball gave bad intelligence that was overstated. Such incidents call for greater oversight of intelligence agencies.

The oversight of intelligence has always been a problem; the ability to control information is an important power in any state. By controlling information, having expertise in surveillance, eavesdropping, and other operations, and by having a cloak of secrecy, an intelligence apparatus has the potential to threaten heads of government. Oversight tends to be the responsibility of executive and legislative powers, and issues are generic: budget, responsiveness to policy needs, quality of analysis, control of operations, and propriety of activities.

GLOSSARY

Noise (intelligence)—Intelligence that includes too much extraneous information and that may hide viable information.

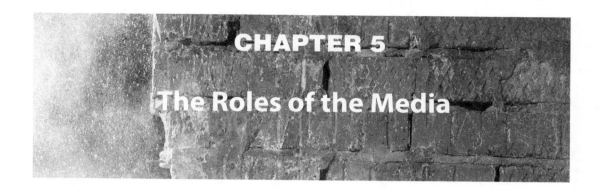

CHAPTER 5

The Roles of the Media

INTRODUCTION

The roles of the media in today's society are diverse and complex in many ways. The media's foremost responsibility is to inform and shape public opinion, but also to connect people and reach a large audience. Media does this by broadcasting on many avenues, including television, radio, print, and Internet. It can be found on billboards, magazine ads, and in movies. Because of the constant

Police tape blocks news reporters from the scene of the Chelsea explosion in New York, 2016.

media saturation in today's day and age, it has become remarkably easy to spread information from one place to another, where once it was more difficult. The media influences many aspects of life, particularly in America. In the realm of homeland security, this can both crucially important and critically dangerous, sometimes both at once. This chapter will review the role of the media in disseminating information and how it can be used as a tool to benefit the population.

LEARNING OUTCOMES

1. Describe the role of the media in a disaster
2. Identify how a population may misinterpret risk

3. Identify the cycles of the media

4. Identify and use the seven rules when dealing with the media

KEY TERMS

Contagion   Framing   Symbiotic

THE MEDIA AND DISASTER PREPAREDNESS

One of the ways that media can be crucially important and critically dangerous is during a period of disaster preparedness. Because the media is in our homes, in our cars, and even in our pockets, it is very easy to reach a number of people in a short amount of time. Information can be a dangerous sword to wield, and it must be handled with care. Often times reporters with little experience or expertise in a specific area will gather information from military and law enforcement officials, and then present it to the public via some sort of broadcast, be it news channels, or Facebook. Their information is not always entirely accurate and is often based off of personal views and conjecture, frequently skewing the reality of a situation. Photographs and videos are shown to the public to illicit emotional responses and are used as a "call to action" for whatever the cause may be.

In crisis, mass media can be a wonderful tool, but it is pertinent to understand several aspects of the media before releasing information. One of those things is the struggle for control of reputation, and the message that's being sent to the viewers. Everybody wants to use the media to his or her own advantage, including the government, interest groups, and terrorists. The more screen time a group has, the more people will be subjected to seeing their intended message, which in turn leads to more action. The theory that "there is no such thing as bad publicity" applies here: even if someone talking badly about something, they're still talking about it. Carlos the Jackal, once one of the world's most wanted terrorists said, "The more I'm talked about, the more dangerous I appear. That's all the better for me." Each group presented via the media wants maximum publicity to be generated by its actions, and aims at intimidation and subjection to attain objections; often times realizing that shock value is high. Timothy McVeigh, the Oklahoma City bomber, was once quoted as saying, "That would not have gotten the point across, we needed a body count to make our point."

The media responds to many facets of life, mostly crises. Economic crisis, such as the financial crisis of 2007–2008, which many economists consider to be the worst financial crisis since the Great Depression, was covered extensively in the news, radio broadcasts, and across numerous web platforms. Criminal crises such as the rise in violence following a Black Lives Matter rally, a law enforcement officer killing a man in what should have been a routine traffic stop, and school shootings are all splashed across media platforms in seconds. Natural disasters such as massive earthquakes and tsunamis are broadcast from all over the world in a rapid fire fashion. Information regarding a political candidate's reputation reaches screens in seconds.

There and benefits and risks associated with this kind of information overload in seconds, however. While it is an asset to be able to communicate with the masses so rapidly, people often hear the "news" via their personal networks, making the issue less of a real-life crisis and more of a personal problem. For example, a man walks into a coffee shop to get a coffee, and the television in the cafe is playing the news channel, which is broadcasting a wildfire. Man hears "wildfire," and calls his wife to tell her about it without being fully informed, because the news is telling him to wait for further details, because it's a "developing story." His wife panics and posts on Facebook about a wildfire, and seven people comment within an hour. The wife tells her friends she's scared, because she has an uncle who lives 3 hours away. The media, the man, and the woman, each, in turn, minimized and mitigated the seriousness of the crisis because of their perceived personal risk. Because the media information outlet but has no real authority on any given subject, they often defer to government officials to be the voice of authority, telling people what to do or how to act in the situation.

In a crisis event, the amount of mass media coverage directly indicates the significance of the crisis. In this way, the media is shaping public opinion by choosing what people are hearing. The availability of accurate, factual information presented by the media can reduce rumor and increase the accuracy of how people assess the situation. Instead, the media often feeds us and encourages viewers to accept isolated, simple facts about the issue, forced to fill in the blanks with their own thoughts and ideas. The way information is presented to people often shapes the way they react to it.

How information in the media is portrayed is called "framing." This theory suggests that how something is presented to the audience influences the choices people make about how to process that information. These frames include: reporting, a short, superficial overview of the facts; dominant, offering only one authority's viewpoints on an issue; conflict, displays both sides of an issue, with expert testimony on both sides; contention, where a variety of opinions and viewpoints are shown to the audience; investigative, where someone exposes corrupt or illegal behavior; campaigning, when the broadcaster is sharing their own personal opinion on a matter; reportage, in-depth coverage of an issue, with detailed background information; community service, providing information for viewers; collective interest to reinforce common values; cultural recognition, a nod to a group's values and norms; and mythic tales, the heartwarming hero stories. How information is presented to the public determines how the public reacts to it.

There are several phases of a crisis for news media. The loss and rescue phase is first. This is the time immediately following a crisis event, where first responders are working to save lives, protect the public, or get the situation under control. Typically, this phase is relatively short, but the loss and rescue phase can be longer, as seen with Hurricane Katrina in 2005. Rescue teams searched for survivors for weeks before the efforts ended and moved onto the second phase, which are damage control and the search for causes. With Hurricane Katrina, the cause was evident: nature. But in cases of reported terrorism, the search for "why" becomes integral at this stage. Damage control presents itself in crises as safe shelters to go to, access to food and water, electricity, and hot water, but also in the form of debates and knee jerk legislation to prevent future events. Once a cause is established, it allows for the third phase: bereavement. This phase is when the citizens bury their dead, and mourn for their losses. It is often highly publicize, like in the wake of the Sandy Hook Elementary School shootings: the funerals were frequented by members of the media, capturing the family's grief as they walked into churches to have services to honor their children. Next, the media brings society into the blame stage, where the culmination of the loss and rescue stage, the damage control and search for causes, and the bereavement stage, target the person or persons responsible. Many times this is shown in the media as a man hunt, or if the person or persons responsible have already been caught, their entire life's story is splashed across news media all over the country. This was shown in the manhunt for Osama Bin Laden following the September 11, 2001 attacks. People in general need someone or something to blame for negative events in their lives, because this ultimately means they can either be exempt from personal blame, or safe moving forward because the threat has been eradicated. After this stage, boredom and confusion sets in. People are no longer interested in hearing about the crisis and are ready for it to "be over." The media reports begin to dwindle down, eventually into nonexistence, except for on the anniversaries of the initial event or crisis. The way the media portrays a crisis also affects terrorists and their methods.

Paul Wilkinson, an expert on terrorism and an Emeritus Professor of International Relations and Director of the University of Saint Andrews Centre for the Study of Terrorism and Political Violence, argues that terrorists use the media to communicate their efforts, using manipulation and exploitation to spread their propaganda. Wilkinson argues that terrorists and mass media have a symbiotic

© Gina Jacobs/Shutterstock.com

The media highly publicized the Sandy Hook shooting mourners.

relationship, one benefits from the other. While most organized terrorist groups have underground communication systems, they still require mainstream media to help spread their messages to more people than they can reach on their own accord. In this way, the mass media serves as an additional psychological weapon for the terrorists, by fostering fear and anxiety in the viewers, often times causing panic. The media may inadvertently shift the blame for terrorist activities to the victims or governments when they report underdeveloped facts or information to the public.

In the event of terrorist activities, the general public is mostly concerned with three things: their personal safety, protection from law enforcement, and the government, and that some entity removes the threat by catching the culprit. This is when mass media implements different "frames," trying to capture the issue from every angle, trying to ensure that everyone hears or sees an issue thoroughly, and that their respective platform gets the most attention. The safety of citizens is directly impacted by the mere existence of mass media in that when people are scared, they will watch the news or read the newspaper, seeking asylum in information, information provided by the same medium that caused the unsettled public. When there is an outcry for public safety and protection, there is also typically a call for action, in this case: catch the terrorist making the threats so that they cease to further threaten the well-being of the nation. In this way, the media is a vicious cycle of cause of effect and can be both damaging and healing.

ISSUES IN THE MEDIA

One of the biggest issues in today's mainstream media is bias. Americans are subjected to many forms of bias in the media, including advertising bias, where the stories are being selected or slanted to please advertisers. Corporate bias is when stories are selected to please the owners of the media venue. Mainstream bias is the tendency of reporting what everyone else is reporting in an effort to avoid news stories that will offend anyone. Sensationalism is a bias in displaying the exceptional occurrences in life over the rare. This is seen when school shootings occur, or an airplane crashes. The media tends to over report these events, making it seem as though they are more common than actual common events, such as hunting accidents or car crashes.

Perhaps the most commonly acknowledged and addressed form of media bias is partisan bias, though. The overwhelming majority of Americans identify as either liberal, or conservative, and the news is no different. It is important to note that one must understand that all news is presented with a bias, or a slant, toward one side of the other. A reporter's job is to report news stories, and reporters are expected to create news frames that directly reflect their outlets orientation. Critics claim that having a liberal bias is anti-Western and anti-American, saying the left wing sympathize with terrorists. Alternately, the critics claim that a conservative bias is dominated by bullies and hatemongers who wish to silence any voice but their own. This display of bias in the mainstream media is impacted by several things, one of which is ownership.

Media ownership is a critical determinant of how news stories are presented and skewed. Most larger mass media enterprises are owned by multinational corporations, making their interests unique, and their bias a financial and economic one. Their intent is to promote the values and goals of business corporations, as the bottom line is the key to their survival. Often times, stories affecting corporate profits are manipulated by the reporters and outlet to reflect these corporations in a positive light, instead of honestly reporting factual information.

Contagion, or the spreading of a harmful idea or practice, is another major issue encountered in the mass media. It is largely unknown what effect increased media has on increased crime rates, but Allan Mazur, a sociologist, engineer, and professor of public affairs at Syracuse University, studied bomb threat in the nuclear industry, and began noting that as news reports of suicide bombings increased, the number of suicide bombings increased as well. Mazur began to wonder if he would find the same pattern in the nuclear industry, and upon further research, discovered that the number of threats proportionately matched the number of news stories. When coverage of bombings increased, the number of bomb threats increased, and when coverage of the bombings diminished, so did the number of bomb threats. From a homeland security perspective, we must decide if it is possible for this trend to be reflected in other situations as well: does additional coverage of mass shootings lead to an increase in mass shootings? Does increased coverage of homicides drive the number of homicides up as well?

One of the consequences of the contagion effect in media reports is that it breeds fear, magnifies threats, therefore causing more threats to spread. M. Cherif Bassiouni, an Emeritus Professor of Law at DePaul University, Consultant to the United States Department of State and the United Nations, states that this media representation influences the way terrorists select their targets and encourages the spread of violence, as they select targets for maximum publicity. Bassiouni noted that there is a connection in the increase of terrorist activities with increased media reporting on it, as well as increased fear among the civilian population. The media drives this fear by continuously reporting on the activities of terrorists or terrorist groups.

The media has priorities in regards to how it deals with the public in the wake of a crisis. First and foremost, they seek to address and consult with those directly affected by the crisis. This can be in the form of testimonials, interviews, etc., to get a "victim impact" of sorts. The information given to reporters has the ability to shape further reports, gather opinions, and form more valid, factual information on what really happened and how people were affected by the event. Immediately following those directly affected by a crisis, the media seeks to speak with the employees, neighbors, families, or any other people indirectly affected by the crisis.

The media operates largely on questions and the inquisitive nature of humans. There is a multifaceted network of questions that circle a media broadcast. One question is: what will the media ask? Because the media are responsible for dispersal of information, they must ask questions to be able to relay

Emergency personnel speak with reporters.

the information to the public. If they pulled up to a motor vehicle accident and did not ask questions, they would be selling conjecture instead of fact. This is true in any crisis situation. Another facet is the general public: what questions will the public have? In order to serve a public, you must understand their desire for knowledge and be able to answer the questions that they want answers to. If the media never answered the public's questions, they would cease to exist. Most of the public is happy with basic information: the who, what, where, when, and why type broadcasts. The government also asks questions before extending information to the media, such as questioning what will the people want to know? How will it affect them? Is it safe, or beneficial to the event or crisis to give out such information? Is it safe for our nation's security to release certain information? The impact of these questions being asked is what is reflected in the media and the information being related.

Crisis involves limited information attention, meaning that the public is served small snippets of information, leaving room for question, and encouraging further attention to the media source and the crisis like a breadcrumb trail. The media's communication efficiency is projected to be roughly 15–20%. Often times their verbal cues do not match their nonverbal communication, such as body language or facial expression. This is intensely noticed by the audience and provides up to 50–75% of message contact. The media often tries to downplay or deny an issue or the trauma caused by it, typically through short message repetition and limiting the numbers of messages given to the public. Their competing agendas between public, private, etc., is often responsible for the emotional arousal of individuals or groups affected by a crisis or event. Another thing that affects how information is given or received is the fear of risk.

"FEAR OF RISK"

Paul Slovic, founder and President of Decision Research, Professor of Psychology at the University of Oregon, and consultant to the government, studies human judgment, risk analysis, and decision-making. Through his studies, Slovic identified that there are some universal perception factors that affect people's responses to a crisis. A few of these perception factors and a short description of each are as follows:

- Control versus no control: An individual or group being able to have control over a situation, versus lacking the ability to control what is happening or is going to happen. This is frequently seen in the event of a natural disaster.

- Immediate/catastrophic versus chronic: This is when an event happens suddenly, as opposed to gradually. This ensures lack of public ability to act on or prepare for an event, thereby causing more panic.

- Natural versus human-made: People in general tend to be less fearful of events that happen or occur naturally than they are of things that we as humans make happen. An example of this is a hurricane, or a mass shooter type situation.

- Risk versus benefit: Most people weigh the risks and benefits of acting upon something. Typically speaking, people tend to have less fear of attempting something or facing something if they receive a benefit even if the outcome is negative, as opposed to pure risk and zero benefit.

- Imposed versus voluntary: When humans are forced against their will to do something, they experience more fear than if they'd voluntarily chosen to do it. The ability to make a decision for oneself can change the way a person reacts to something.

- Trust versus distrust: This is perhaps the most important perception. Being in the company of a person who is trustworthy can encourage another person to be less fearful in a situation. When a person is with someone they do not trust, their level of fear is more intense. The less fearful an individual is, the more likely they are to react positively to a stimulus.

These perceptions are reflected in the way that people respond or react to a news broadcast, an event, or crisis.

CYCLES OF MEDIA

Following any event, the media works in cycles. On the first day, the media releases their initial statement quickly, offering any details that they may deem important or necessary. They will be present and reporting at initial news conferences and interviews with government or city officials. The challenge on day one becomes rumor management and trying to control the flow of information released to the public. On days two and three, the media strives to make supportive experts available for interviews. This can be to confirm what they're reporting, or to support their information. Often times, the challenge on these days becomes the balance of expectations and using past events or behaviors as a way to explain predicted future actions. Day four and beyond, victims and families may begin to feel bitter and intruded upon, and the challenge for the media then becomes still attempting to gather information from unwilling sources and keeping the story in the news.

There are "Seven Rules" for the media that should be followed at all costs to maintain trust and solidarity between the media and the citizens in a country. Rule 1: Accept and involve the public as a legitimate partner. If the public is involved in the media, reports will be more centered toward what the public wants, needs, or thinks, making the media an even stronger asset to the community. Rule 2: Plan carefully and evaluate your efforts. The value of proper planning when it comes to security and dealing with the public should not be underestimated. To ensure that all broadcasts are well planned, and carefully evaluated following their broadcasts, assures that future broadcasts will likely reach more people because the integrity of the media is intact. Rule 3: Listen to the public's specific concerns. By listening to the concerns of the people who value the work and patronize the media by returning to watch, listen, or read their reports, you are ensuring that they will return and continue to do so by making them feel heard. Rule 4: Be honest, frank, and open. Do not try to minimize an issue by being dishonest, but neither should the media exacerbate an issue by publishing misinformation. Rule 5: Coordinate and collaborate with other credible sources. Professionals, government officials, and other credible sources of information should be included in media reports, so the information is presented in the most honest, intelligent means available. Rule 6: Meet the needs of the media and public. The media needs the public viewers to survive, and in turn, the public needs the media to be accurately informed of the goings on in the country and the world. Both are dependent on one another in some capacity. Rule 7: Speak clearly and with compassion. The reporters who are concise and compassionate with their reporting have higher ratings and are favored by the general public over those who do not speak clearly, who do not seem compassionate to the situation they are reporting on, and can often times cause a disparity in the viewing groups because of this. In order to maintain a trustworthy, accurate portrayal of events, the news media must do these seven things in order to maintain personal and professional integrity.

Because the media plays such a large role in today's society, it is important that all aspects of the media are considered, analyzed, and properly handled, particularly in the realm of homeland security. Information in the wrong hands could be fatal.

GLOSSARY

Contagion—The spreading of a harmful idea or practice.

Framing—The theory suggests that how something is presented to the audience influences the choices people make about how to process that information.

Symbiotic—Having an interdependent relationship.

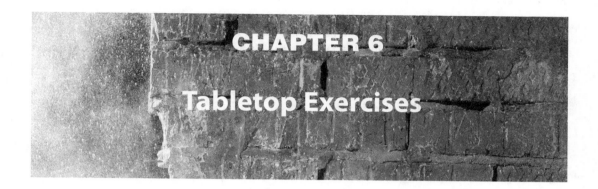

CHAPTER 6
Tabletop Exercises

INTRODUCTION

Tabletop exercises provide a means by which leaders and responders can practice the techniques to handle a threat, crisis, or incident, also known as a Undesirable Event (**UDE**). The process of managing any UDE has a basic structure. The process can be identified in the following steps:

A bomb squad robot inspects a suspicious backpack.

1. Identify what are the immediate threats—what is the next outcome that would cause the greatest harm?

2. What or who are at risk of being harmed if the next threat becomes a reality?

3. Can we prevent the harm? If so, what is the safest process to do so?

4. Go back to Step 1 and assess the next highest threat. This cycle continues until no significant threats exist.

The above process can be used before, during, and after a UDE. Before the UDE, the process can prevent loss and protect the greatest assets. Usually, humans are the greatest asset, thus our first concern is how to protect people. This may mean that those in danger must evacuate an area or it may be that they stay in place. For example, if a bomb threat was received for an office building, our first step may be to evacuate the building quickly and efficiently. Employees should take the fastest route without putting them closer to the improvised explosive device (**IED**). On the other hand, if the threat is an **active shooter** in an office building, those in offices and rooms should **shelter in place**, unlike an IED the shooter is likely moving. If you ordered an evacuation, the evacuees could inadvertently confront the shooter.

LEARNING OUTCOMES

1. Comprehend the process of identifying the threats
2. Assess what is the greatest risk on a given incident
3. Describe a method to reduce the threat
4. Able to follow the steps of mitigating a threat during a UDE

KEY TERMS

Active shooter	HVAC	UDE
Field exercises	IED	Shelter in place

Review of each step of the process will shed light on the process:

Step 1: Identify the Immediate Threats

The process of identifying the threat may seem simple, but depending on the situation the threat may not be so obvious. In the case of an IED, the threat is an explosion. It is important to remember that the size of the IED changes how you may respond. In some cases the IED's construction is unknown so you must expect worst-case scenario. That may be explosive, biological/chemical, or both. If the IED is in an open field, the threat of the explosion would be far less than the threat of a chemical attack. On the other hand, if the IED is in the basement of a building, the threat of explosion may be greater than the chemical threat because the chemical would become trapped in the basement (as long as a heating, ventilation, air-conditioning system (**HVAC**) system does not pull air from the basement). In addition, even if the incident is over, additional hazards may remain. For example, after a hurricane has passed, power lines, damaged buildings, and hazardous water may be the greatest threats to the population.

Knowing more about your threat, that is, what it is and how it is constructed, and your environment will drive what you determine to be your greatest threat. The variety of possibilities is endless; therefore, the tabletop exercise method is most effective in practicing the method of risk mitigation. Practice using a variety of threats such as a vehicle IED outside a government building, unknown package in a shopping center, a leaked container of a chemical from a shipping container, or an active shooter on a university campus. Each scenario should challenge participants to think through the potential threats. This step should not be confused with the next step. A natural tendency is to think about the victims or what could be damaged while considering the threat. Participants must fight the urge to move into Step 2, known as "tunnel vision," because it causes the participant to forget any other aspects of the scenario. With tunnel vision, the participant focuses too much on one threat and forgets that other threats and possibilities exist. This step is largely done by the incident commander but others may assist in this process. Once all threats, or what is known of them, have been identified, the incident commander can move to Step 2.

Step 2: What Is the Greatest Risk?

Once the threats have been identified, those or what at risk can be identified. Generally, humans are of the greatest value. Although we often consider this to be obvious, the logic of this is more than simply that we don't want people to die or get hurt. When the public, customers, or employees are harmed, the responsible party will be liable for costs associated with that harm. For example, if a group of employees at an office are killed in an explosion, the business may be responsible for those lives and may spend years in court explaining their role in the deaths. Costs of a loss in life can easily top the cost of a building. Situations do arise when certain lives are worthless than others. For example, when members of the Secret Service are tasked with protecting the President, Vice President, or dignitaries, their lives are considered to be an acceptable loss for the life of their protectee. It is in essence their job to put their own lives at risk for another. That said, all life should be protected and responders should not put a life in danger if another option is possible. For example, bomb technicians will use a robot to inspect a device instead of a person even though bomb technicians are very aware of the risks of the job.

It is important to refrain from tunnel vision by identifying the greatest of risks. Certainly people will be at the top of your list if humans are in peril, but is there equipment or additional hazards that should be addressed? For example, if a hospital is the target of an IED, are biological hazards that could also be a threat. If so, you should be sure to go back to Step 1 with this threat. Some

A robot inspects a suspicious package.

equipment is so specialized that it is worth saving. For example, if a laboratory with specialized equipment for research is at risk, it may be worth the effort to protect it if it does not put lives at risk. This process can be used before an incident to reduce risk if an incident were ever to occur. For example, a business may choose to distribute key functions, such as data servers and leadership, to reduce the overall impact should an incident occur without adversely affecting productivity. A key consideration is how mobile the asset before or during an incident. Moving your asset may be the quickest way to reduce risk. Once the greatest risks have been identified and prioritized, then Step 3 can be begun.

Step 3: Reducing the Threat

Starting with the greatest asset, determine a method to reduce the risk. This may be as simple as moving the asset. For example, a good plan for an IED in an office building may be to call for an evacuation. An evacuation moves the asset of humans away from the threat. If the IED is in an empty park, no significant asset may be worth saving. In this case, a planned detonation in the park maybe the best choice because render the IED safe would put personnel at unnecessary risk. In the case of an active shooter in a shopping mall, the threat is the shooter and the asset is people. The best plan to reduce the risk may be for shoppers to shelter in place in stores then close off entry into the store. Blocking the shooter reduces the risk to the shoppers; when compared to the risk that shoppers may face if they tried to evacuate, it may be the wisest choice. It would likely be best if the threat in this case was neutralized. Thus, a team of well-armed and trained personnel may be tasked to eliminate the threat. Consider if this team ran across a victim who has been shot. Should the team stop and help the victim? If you thought about how the shooter may be harming others and how rendering first aid would delay eliminating the threat, you are following the correct line of thought. What may seem counterintuitive may be the best option for the safety of others.

Deciding what is best for any situation means considering a variety of options. This is where a good analysis and planning team is critical. The incident commander may be able to make all decisions for a small-scale incident, but as the incident becomes larger and more widespread, the number of decisions that need to be made grows exponentially. A team of people that assist the incident commander will be critical for large-scale incident. Although major decisions must be made by the incident commander, an analysis and planning team can provide the correct information to help the commander make a quick yet wise decision.

What decisions are best is never clear until the incident is over. Each incident commander will make a different set of choices but the ultimate outcome may be the same. Thus, it is important that team members respect the decisions of an incident commander. All team members should respect another team member's role, and it is important to keep egos aside. Tabletop exercises should be practiced often for team members to become accustomed with each other. Respecting one another would be ideal, but respecting the decisions of another is vital for operations to continue.

Once a plan to mitigate loss is identified and put into action, the next greatest threat and corresponding risk can be addressed. The process continues until the incident has reached a point that it is no longer a crisis. Long-term recovery can then take place. This may be rebuilding a township, coxing an economy to function again, or helping employees trust that they are safe at work. To accomplish long-term goals, a robust feedback and response mechanism is the key. Each incident is different, so each incident must be and will be managed differently. Ultimately, as long as the greatest of assets, people, are safe and the rest can be sorted out.

WHY USE TABLETOPS?

The general process, as outlined in the previous pages, gives a framework for commanders and leaders to follow. Participants in a tabletop take on roles. In the field, these roles would be taken by those who work in that area. Thus, police operations should be represented by a police chief, lieutenant, or sergeant. But in the classroom the roles of the Emergency Operations Center (EOC) should be distributed to teams. In addition, students should be familiar with all roles of the EOC.

Agencies, departments, and civilians act in tabletops to test capabilities, practice the process of working together, and find weaknesses. Each set of participants set a different dynamic and have weaknesses. In the real world, that weakness might be a personnel or equipment deficiency. It may be that the radios are not correctly encrypted or that responders cannot effectively communicate. Often civilians are not familiar with radio language or discipline. This is one example of how tabletops help identify weaknesses and develop the team. If your first real incident is the first time that team members have worked with one another, expect that the incident response will be challenging. Thus, practice is critical.

Tabletop exercises can range from short to rather long exercises. Generally, teams that have to work together work more efficiently. In addition, those that have had exposure to the tabletop process are also less likely to fumble and exercise. Students have an opportunity to learn the process and appreciate all roles before having to work in a department or agency. This type of previous experience can be invaluable for employers who will depend on these new employees to take up the job of an experienced employee. Personal development and learning how to work as a team are an important aspect of tabletops. Participants should come to the tabletop with an open mind and a willingness to learn from each other.

The cost of a tabletop can be very low but the cost in time can be considerable but certainly worth it. From this perspective, tabletops are a very efficient because they work well and cost very little. Although **field exercises** would be optimal because it fully tests out personnel, not just leaders, and the equipment, they can be very costly and time consuming. It is advised that all responding teams conduct a field exercise at least once a year. Policies developed from tabletops or field exercises are the ultimate purpose of these training strategies in the real world. Participants should keep notes on what the weak points of their agency is and what can be done to make future real or tabletop incidents run more smoothly.

IN THE CLASSROOM

Students have a considerable opportunity to build skills and abilities that agencies and departments need to function. The process of a tabletop in an educational institution offers considerable benefit to learning it on the job. The following are highly encouraged during tabletops in the classroom:

Conduct at least three tabletop exercises in a term:

The more practice that students get, the better. That said, the first tabletop for students is generally very stressful for the students and frustrating for the instructor. It is suggested that a simple incident is used for the first attempt. Students should focus on their role and instructors should watch for strong and weak personalities. Stronger personalities may try to influence or even detract from the roles of others. Weaker personalities will allow a stronger partner to carry the team. Each team member must add to the experience within their role. Second, a third tabletop will establish a healthy working relationship.

Randomly assign roles:

When conducting the tabletops, EOC teams should be randomly assigned into roles. In addition, team members should also be randomly assigned. Thus, the likelihood that two students will have worked together and that any one student has the same role as a previous exercise should be low. Instructors can also choose to assign the roles so as to ensure that all students get a varied experience. Furthermore, running more exercises will ensure that students truly get a wide set of experiences.

Run small teams:

Classes that are larger can be broken into two separate EOCs with two different scenarios. Roles in the teams should be limited to three students maximum. Roles made up of one individual are optimal and roles of two can also be beneficial to create team cohesion. Additional instructors can be used to maintain the scenario for each team.

Classroom roles can be different than real life:

In the real world, participants act as their role in real life. Thus, the chief of police would act in his role within the EOC. In the classroom, roles can be very similar to mimic the real world. Alternatively, instructors may choose to center on duties in the EOC rather than jobs that make up the EOC. Here is a breakdown of roles for the EOC:

Incident Commander
Elected Officials
Town Managers
Health Department
Firefighting Support
Law Enforcement
Attorney's Office
Emergency Medical Services

The above set of roles focuses on the job of individuals in the EOC. This is very representative of how the EOC is made up in the real world. In the classroom another method can be used to more clearly define the tasks of the EOC itself. The following roles can be used as an alternative:

Incident Commander
Planning and Analysis
Population Protection
External Coordination
Facility and Equipment Mobilization
Communications and Media Relations
Recovery
Lessons Learned and Policy

Exercise planning can be completed by a predesigned incident script. FEMA has several such scripts available. These scenarios can be very detailed and some contain fictitious maps. Instructors can also choose to create their own using their own locality, for example, creating a scenario at the local government building or shopping center. In both cases, the students are able to practice their skills in emergency and risk management. If scenarios are tailors around the area that the students live and work, an added benefit may be that they learn helpful lessons for their future employment. Drafting a scenario can be detailed or general with experience running tabletops as an asset in either case. Having an instructor or a leader who has experience doing tabletops will help work through the initial confusion. It is typical that a team that has never used the tabletop process will manage the incident poorly, become frustrated with each other, and may result in a complete failure.

Exercise Planning

The key components of exercise planning are to establish objectives. This may be to validate plans or to assemble key players. Establishing a timeline is important to give participants an idea of how long operations may take to complete. In the real world, emergency operations a quite a bit of hurry up then wait. During tabletops, it may be important to help participants learn this, but a compressed timeline can help getting the most from the time of participants. One such example of a compressed timeline is to set a ratio such as 10 minutes is equal to 1 hour.

Each scenario, however, devised should have a set of rules. In the classroom, this can be points deducted for "harming the population" or "delaying a decision." Evaluation of the tabletop is critical for the team to get better. Feedback on what was done correctly and incorrectly can dramatically improve performance. To improve performance, participants should complete FEMA training such as IS100, IS200, and IS700. The following chapters will review the procedures for a tabletop in each of the following scenarios: explosive device, chemical or biological agent/device, and nuclear/radiological.

GLOSSARY

Active Shooter—An individual who is walking and firing a weapon at victims, generally small arms.

Field Exercises—In contrast to a tabletop, these exercises are done physically. Generally, these exercises are done outside will all first responders and leadership participating. Simulations are limited as personnel should become familiar with equipment.

HVAC—Heating, ventilation, air-conditioning system.

IED—(improvised explosive device)-This is a bomb designed by some criminal or terrorist individual or group. Varieties that use biological or chemical agents are identified as chemical IEDs or biological IEDs. Those using nuclear material are Improvised Nuclear Devices or IND.

UDE—(undesirable event)-This is the event that the team is attempting to prevent. In the case of an IED, the UDE is the uncontrolled detonation of the IED.

Shelter in place—Stay in the room that the victims may be located with the door locked and possibly staying in the furthest corner from the door.

CHAPTER 7

Tabletop Exercises—Biological and Chemical

CHEMICAL INCIDENT

Applicability and Scope

Tabletop exercises designed for emergency response to terrorism offer opportunities to apply the principles of prevention, protection, mitigation, response, and recovery. Tabletop exercises in the classroom setting provide students the ability to systematically talk through various scenarios. The following chemical agent scenario should result in conducting an on scene threat assessment to determine the complexity of the incident and the level of response required. This scenario should lead to identifying the level of threat, resources needed, protection measures required, mitigation or neutralization options, and recovery requirements. The scope of this exercise is to open discuss with prompts from a moderator's questions.

Purpose

The purpose of this tabletop exercise is to examine current policies, procedures, resources, and actions in the context of a chemical dispersal device. This exercise

© ChameleonsEye/Shutterstock.com

Israeli emergency forces carry out an exercise which simulates a chemical and biological rocket attack.

should also promote greater understanding and ability to apply NIMS/ICS principles. This exercise should identify what went well and identify what went wrong in a hot wash setting and result in participants making recommended improvements.

LEARNING OUTCOMES

1. Evaluate policies and procedures as outlined in local, state, or federal response plans, to evaluate command and control in the Incident Command construct
2. Identify resources needed versus available by applying the concept of on the scene threat analysis to determine response requirements
3. Identifying response through recovery procedures
4. Enhance understanding of concepts in an emergency response scenario from all stake holders' perspectives

Rules/Conduct

The intent of a tabletop exercise is to create dialogue about various issues in relation to a given scenario. Participants are encouraged to collectively explore in depth the various aspects of the event. Ground rules for a tabletop exercise and open dialogue require creativity and group problem solving. Participants are encouraged to foster active thinking, active listening, and active participation. Most importantly, the group must respect one another; challenge the ideas not the people. Participants must be encouraged to contribute and understand there is no admonishment for incorrect decisions.

- Reference: Homeland Security Exercise and Evaluation Program (2013). Department of Homeland Security, retrieved from https://www.fema.gov/media-library/assets/documents/32326

Tabletops in the classroom generally assume that the following have been met:

- National Incident Management System implemented
- Municipality has the required resources for response
- Municipality has standard governmental structure
- Affected entity has contingency plans unless the scenario dictates otherwise

Scenario Overview

The local shoe manufacturing company is a 20,000 square foot facility. The entrance is a typical entrance for any business consisting of double glass front doors and a reception area immediately upon entering. The reception area is a containment area with one entry past the receptionist. The receptionist sits behind a greeting counter. To gain entrance, individuals must pass through the receptionist with a badge. Once granted entry, the hallway takes individuals to the office area. Past the office area is the main manufacturing floor. Workers for the assembly line have a back entrance that requires a PIN code for access. The entire facility is monitored with closed circuit monitors and recorded on a cloud storage network.

- On the morning of July 23, 2013 at 0800 hours, workers were beginning to show up for their shift at the local shoe manufacturing company. Their shift begins at 0830. In the male locker room where workers typically change into their uniforms and store their personal belongings, a worker noticed a suspicious looking card board box in the corner of the locker room. It seemed out of place.

- The worker approached noticing the flaps were open on top. Curious, the worker opened the top of the box and noticed what appeared to be a gas cylinder lying on top of sticks of dynamite with wires protruding from the dynamite.

- Panicking, the worker began to notify others in locker room. Approximately 15 workers began to evacuate the locker room. Remembering his training about bomb threats, the worker initiated the company's contingency plan for bomb scenarios. He began verbally notifying other workers while simultaneously notifying security and passing along what he witnessed. At 0807, security called 911. The shoe plant continued with implementing its evacuation plan.

- 911 received the call, and immediately notified the jurisdictional fire and police department and relayed the pertinent information about the dynamite and cylinder.

- At 0812, the fire department arrives and notices the plant still evacuating. They establish an upwind entry control point due to the information about a gas cylinder. The fire department also initiated Incident Command (IC) and requested the police to establish a XXX foot cordon.

- The IC seeks out the plant authorities.

- At 0818, the IC tracks down plant security and requests them to find the individual who discovered the suspicious package. The IC establishes liaison with plant officials to facilitate informational requests. The IC confirms the shoe plant is evacuated and the bomb squad is en-route.

- At 0825, plant security returns with the witness who discovered the device. The IC still waiting for the bomb squad to arrive begins questioning the witness.

- At this point of the scenario, the concept of conducting an on scene threat assessment may be prudent. Using what was covered in Chapter 9 and the concepts of NIMS, the group should open discuss what the IC should be considering.

Key Questions

- What is the scope of the threat?
- Should the IC activate the EOC?
- What resources are still required?
- What elements about the device are unknown?
  - What can be observed with the witness that discovered the device?
- Critical infrastructure?
- Will this knowledge help the IC formulate a better plan?
- What else should the IC plan for?
  - Who else needs to be notified?
    - Federal agencies?
  - Further evacuation?
  - Public Affairs?
  - Utilities impacted?
  - Potential hazards?

Resumption of Scenarios

- At 0835, the IC concludes questioning the witness and security. The IC was able to obtain additional information not previously known. After conducting an on scene threat assessment, the IC was able to conclude that the workers in the locker room were the likely intended target. Further device details include, it was three sticks of dynamite measuring approximately six inches long by one inch diameter. The IC also determined access to this area is controlled by employees using a PIN to gain access. Additionally, the IC has ascertained that there is no critical infrastructure or significant hazards that may be impacted. Based on the information from the witness, the IC has decided the current cordon is sufficient pending for the bomb squad's analysis. At this point, the IC does not see the necessity of activating the EOC or evacuating any further beyond the shoe plant itself.

- At 0840, the bomb squad arrives. The team, being part-time patrol and part-time bomb squad had to be recalled; response times can be significant. The bomb squad commander makes contact with the IC.

- At 0845, the IC briefs the bomb squad on the known information. Based on this information, the team begins formulating a plan. The team commander recommends the cordon is satisfactory and does not recommend additional evacuations in neighboring businesses; the commander suggests that these neighboring businesses shelter in place and to stay away from windows. The closest business to the shoe plant is 700 feet downwind. This business is an auto repair facility with multiple garage bays with the doors open.

- The team commander must also question the witness and plant security. In the interim, the bomb squad team members begin equipment preparation.

- At 0855, the team commander concludes additional questioning (Reference Witness Questioning Guide Chapter 9). Based on the questioning, the commander was able to add to the information obtained by the IC. Significantly, it was determined that there is video surveillance available. It was also ascertained the shoe company had fired a worker earlier in the week, and this individual was suspected of making telephonic threats. It was also determined that the witness was not displaying any symptoms after opening the box. The team commander decided that it was necessary to track down the individual who was fired, obtain a background check on this individual, and also get access to the video surveillance.

- The shoe plant security informed the commander that the surveillance video is stored on a cloud and is accessible via the Internet. Using Wi-Fi, they were able to view the video. The suspect was observed entering the assembly line employee entrance at 0745. He was observed carrying a card board box approximately 1 foot high by 2 feet wide. There is no video in the men's locker room. The suspect was observed departing the same path entered at 0749. Security confirmed that it is the individual who was recently fired.

- The commander relays this information to IC and emphasizes the urgency to track down the individual seen on the video. Patrols are sent to last known address.

- At 0900, the team makes initial entry for reconnaissance using their robot.

- At 0910, the bomb squad has video eyes on the device via their robot. On the cylinder, they see a label with this information and symbols:

- **Shipping Name:** Chlorine
- **Identification Number:** 1017 (Guide 124)
- **Hazardous Class or Division:** 2.3
- **Subsidiary Hazardous Class or Division:** 8
- **Label:** Poison, Inhalation Hazard Corrosive Toxic Gas

- Reference: http://www.cdc.gov/niosh/ershdb/EmergencyResponseCard_29750024. html

- At 0915, a patrol makes contact with suspect at last known address and detains individual for questioning. The patrol notices items of interest in the open at suspect's home. On the kitchen table are random "how to" anarchist books. Also out in the open are additional gas cylinders.

Key Questions

- What additional threat assessment can be determined based on the questioning of the witness?

- What can be determined by a background check on the suspect?

- What intelligence can be gathered at the suspect's residence?

- Can the suspect be questioned? What legal parameters must be followed?

- What elements of threat assessment can be determined?
  - Agent?
  - Target?
  - Vulnerability (ease of access)?
  - Intent?
  - Capability?
  - Potential damage?

- What is still unknown?

- What new actions if any are required by the IC?

Resumption of Scenarios

- At 0918, the bomb squad is finishing reconnaissance with the robot. Using the video camera, they were able to determine the device was set up on a timer using a small battery powered analog clock. They were able to determine that the cylinder is approximately the size of a 2-liter pressure bottle.

- The IC and bomb squad commander decide to formulate a plan of attack. Due to the discovery of the timer, the bomb squad commander does not want to make a manual entry. Based on their analysis, they feel the cylinder can be removed by the robot eliminating the contents as a threat.

- At 0930, as the robot was picking up the cylinder, the cylinder dispensed its contents.

- The door to the locker room was propped open when the robot made entry. Additionally the assembly line employee entrance was propped open to facilitate the robot's entry and exit.
- A slight yellowish cloud billows out the door and begins to quickly dissipate.
- With the cylinder still in the grippers of the robot, the commander directs the robot driver to move the cylinder away from the explosive device.

Key Questions

- What hazards exist with chlorine gas?
- Is there a threat concerning any gas that escaped the employee entrance?
- What should the IC be planning for?

Resumption of Scenarios

- An explosive hazard still exists. At 0940, the bomb squad commander decides a render safe procedure must be conducted on the remaining device. Using standard procedures, the bomb squad disarmed the device.
- At 1000, the commander briefs the IC that the device is safe; however, there are still residual hazards.
  - Contents of cylinder must be confirmed
  - The remnants of the container must be packaged
  - The shoe plant is contaminated
  - There are explosive components remaining

Key Questions

- How should recovery proceed?
- What evidence should be recovered?
- What federal agencies if any should be involved?
- What resources are needed for recovery?

Hot Wash

- What could the IC have done better?
- What went well?

BIOLOGICAL INCIDENT

Applicability and Scope

Tabletop exercises designed for emergency response to terrorism offer opportunities to apply the principles of prevention, protection, mitigation, response, and recovery. Tabletop exercises in the classroom setting provide students the ability to systematically talk through various scenarios. The following biological agent scenario should result in conducting an on scene threat assessment to determine the complexity of the incident and the level of response required. This scenario should lead to identifying the level of threat, resources needed, protection measures required, mitigation or neutralization options, and recovery requirements. The scope of this exercise is to open discuss with prompts from a moderator's questions.

Purpose

The purpose of this tabletop exercise is to examine current policies, procedures, resources, and actions in the context of a biological incident. This exercise should also promote greater understanding and ability to apply NIMS/ICS principles. This exercise should identify what went well and identify what went wrong in a hot wash setting and result in participants making recommended improvements.

Consideration for this tabletop exercise should be given to the intent vice the actual plausibility or effectiveness of a biological attack. The purpose of this tabletop is to exercise the response to a National level event, not dispute whether or not it could actually happen. Every attempt was made to ensure certain levels of realism and preserve certain levels of plausibility.

Objectives

The objective of this scenario is to evaluate policies and procedures as outlined in local, state, or federal response plans, to evaluate command and control in the IC construct, and to identify resources needed versus available by applying the concept of on scene threat analysis to determine response requirements. Additional objectives may include identifying response through recovery procedures. The overall objective of this biological scenario is to enhance understanding of the unique dynamics involving the use of a biological agent. Participants should depart this scenario with a keen sense of the time delay in recognizing a terrorist attack using a biological agent and the prospects of this type of scenario being a National level event.

- Reference: Homeland Security Exercise and Evaluation Program (2013). Department of Homeland Security, retrieved from https://www.fema.gov/media-library/assets/documents/32326

Rules/Conduct

The intent of a tabletop exercise is to create dialogue about various issues in relation to a given scenario. Participants are encouraged to collectively explore in depth the various aspects of the event. Ground rules for a tabletop exercise and open dialogue require creativity and group problem solving. Participants are encouraged to foster active thinking, active listening, and active participation. Most importantly, the group must respect one another; challenge the ideas not the people. Participants must be encouraged to contribute and understand there is no admonishment for incorrect decisions.

Tabletops in the classroom generally assume that the following have been met:

- National Incident Management System implemented
- Municipality has the required resources for response
- Municipality has standard governmental structure
- Affected entity has contingency plans unless the scenario dictates otherwise

Background Considerations for a Biological Attack

- There are few examples for emergency responders to refer to concerning the actual use of biological agent in a terrorist attack. As previously discussed, the use of biological agent is plausible but the reality of its use as an effective terrorist tool is yet to be seen. There are many variables why biological agents are dismissed as a method of attack. These include but not limited to: obtaining a lethal agent, in certain cases—manufacturing limitations, effective employment—stability of the agent, and many others. Just the same, there are advantages to using biological agents: cheap production, vast dissemination potential, mass public fear, and they can be employed undetected.

- A main consideration for emergency responders is the delay of symptoms. Most biological agents will not manifest for 24–72 hours. With this type of delay, the fact that this may be a terrorist attack may go unnoticed, initially. The scope and scale of the attack are what Emergency Planners must be prepared for. The following exercise is intended to provoke thought and discussion based on a National level crisis. It stands to reason for maximum effectiveness, fear generation, and economic impact; terrorists would employ a toxin on a grandeur scale than a local municipality.

- Due to the lapse of recognizing an attack and subsequent symptoms, the use of an on scene threat assessment may not be prudent or useful for this type of scenario. One must consider the method of deployment of the toxin. If an organization is to take the time and make the investment to develop a toxin, they will ensure that it is disseminated more surreptitiously and effectively than what a lone wolf may employ.

■ "Even small-scale attacks, however, could be highly lethal and disruptive, and as has been noted, there is a real possibility of a campaign of bioattacks on multiple targets (the "reload" phenomenon)—because some of these weapons are self-replicating organisms. Moreover, it is not necessary for a nation-state to maintain a large stockpile of bioweapons as the development of a significant offensive bioattack capability could occur within weeks or months." As quoted by—Written testimony of OHA acting Assistant Secretary Dr. Kathy Brinsfield and S&T Under Secretary Dr. Reginald Brothers for a House Committee on Homeland Security, Subcommittee on Emergency Preparedness, Response, and Communications hearing titled "BioWatch: Lessons Learned and the Path Forward"

■ Reference: http://www.dhs.gov/news/2014/06/10/
written-testimony-oha-acting-assistant-secretary-and-st-under-secretary-house

Scenario Overview

There has been recognized "chatter" in various terrorist media outlets on the discussion of using biological agents against the United States. This has caught the attention of U.S. intelligence agencies. Subsequently, there have been many reports published to discuss the veracity of the increased chatter about biological agent. Emergency planners across the Nation are receiving intelligence bulletins from fusion cells and various federal agencies about the potential use of biological agents by terrorist organizations. Most of the discussion in the intelligence reports indicates an interest by terrorists to employ a food-borne agent.

Key Questions

■ What resources are available for Emergency Planners, Law Enforcement, and other stakeholders to enhance their knowledge of biological response requirements?

■ Considering the intelligence updates, what should municipalities, Emergency Management be doing?

Resumption of Scenarios

As a key stakeholder in an emergency response to a biological attack, you have completed some research. Based on the intelligence, you researched the CDC for information on biological agents and discovered the CDC categorizes agents based on criticality A through C. See Table 7.1 that categorizes biological agents. This table consists of identified "Agents of Concern".

Table 7.1

Category A

The U.S. public health system and primary health-care providers must be prepared to address varied biological agents, including pathogens that are rarely seen in the United States. High-priority agents include organisms that pose a risk to national security because they

- can be easily disseminated or transmitted person-to-person;
- cause high mortality, with potential for major public health impact;
- might cause public panic and social disruption; and
- require special action for public health preparedness (Box 2).

Category A, agents include
- variola major (smallpox);
- *Bacillus anthracis* (anthrax);
- *Yersinia pestis* (plague);
- *Clostridium botulinum toxin* (botulism);
- *Francisella tularensis* (tularaemia);
- filoviruses,
    - —Ebola hemorrhagic fever,
    - —Marburg hemorrhagic fever; and
- arenaviruses,
    - —Lassa (Lassa fever),
    - —Junin (Argentine hemorrhagic fever) and related viruses.

Category B

Second highest priority agents include those that

- are moderately easy to disseminate;
- cause moderate morbidity and low mortality; and
- require specific enhancements of CDC's diagnostic capacity and enhanced disease surveillance.

Category B agents include
- *Coxiella burnetti* (Q fever);

(continued)

- *Brucella species* (brucellosis);
- *Burkholderia mallei* (glanders);
- alphaviruses,
  —Venezuelan encephalomyelitis,
  —eastern and western equine encephalomyelitis;
- ricin toxin from *Ricinus communis* (castor beans);
- epsilon toxin of *Clostridium perfringens*; and
- *Staphylococcus* enterotoxin B.

A subset of List B agents includes pathogens that are food- or waterborne. These pathogens include but are not limited to

- *Salmonella* species,
- *Shigella dysenteriae*,
- *Escherichia coli* O157:H7,
- *Vibrio cholerae*, and
- *Cryptosporidium parvum*.

Category C
Third highest priority agents include emerging pathogens that could be engineered for mass dissemination in the future because of

- availability;
- ease of production and dissemination; and
- potential for high morbidity and mortality and major health impact.

Category C agents include
- Nipah virus,
- hantaviruses,
- tickborne hemorrhagic fever viruses,
- tickborne encephalitis viruses,
- yellow fever, and
- multidrug-resistant tuberculosis.

Preparedness for List C agents requires ongoing research to improve disease detection, diagnosis, treatment, and prevention. Knowing in advance which newly emergent pathogens might be employed by terrorists is not possible; therefore, linking bioterrorism preparedness efforts with ongoing disease surveillance and outbreak response activities as defined in CDC's emerging infectious disease strategy is imperative.[1]

---

[1] CDC, Preventing emerging infectious diseases: a strategy for the 21st century. Atlanta, Georgia: U.S. Department of Health and Human Services, 1998.

- Reference: Centers for Disease Control and Prevention. Biological and Chemical Terrorism: Strategic Plan for Preparedness and Response. Recommendations of the CDC Strategic Planning Workgroup. MMWR 2000;49(No. RR-4):[inclusive page numbers].

Scenario Continued: Of the agents of concern, Emergency Planners should extrapolate the most likely agent to be used in a food-borne attack. Research reveals from the list, *Clostridium botulinum* as the most probable agent for a food-borne attack.

- Federal agencies continue to disperse intelligence bulletins. Of note, many refer back to the *Salmonella typhimurium* attack in Dalles, Oregon; using this event as an example and lesson learned. This attack is of particular importance as it is the first known mass exposure of a U.S. populace to an intentional biological attack. In September of 1984, Rajneeshee cult members intentionally contaminated Dalles area salad bars with Salmonella. Seven hundred fifty are sickened and 40 are placed in the hospital. The Rajneesh cult was attempting to influence a local election by reducing the potential voting populace. Intelligence bulletins highlight that this event went undetected for a year and was only identified when cult members turned informants.

- Reference: Cordesman, A., Burke A., (2005, May). The Challenge of Biological Terrorism: When to Cry Wolf, What to Cry and How to Cry It. Center for Strategic and International Studies, CSIS.Org.

Key Questions

- Based on the lesson learned and the intelligence bulletins, what private sectors should Emergency Management be working with?
- What resources should the Federal government be preparing? What is available?
- What should Law Enforcement agencies be concerned with? Are there precursors LE should be aware of?
- What should hospitals be aware of? What is their role?

Scenario Continued: A well-organized terrorist group has emplaced cells in all 50 states. This group has recruited a dozen biological scientists with various backgrounds. This terrorist group has a long history of trying attacks that are often dismissed by other groups. This group is well funded; they have engaged in global criminal networks for years and have built a solid network of funding. They have a goal of economically collapsing the United States. There is nothing within their ideology that will limit what methods of attack they will use.

- This terrorist group has also reviewed and adapted tactics and techniques from the Rajneesh attack. Additionally, they have thoroughly reviewed empirical data from the Aum Shinrikyo events in Japan. This event was an important lesson for the terrorist group as it highlights the possibilities. The Aum Shinrikyo's biological program faltered and resulted in being useless; however, their chemical program arguably was a success. The terrorist group was able to extract lessons from the Shinrikyo's failures; they garnered valuable lesson from the failed biological program and learned from the Rajneesh successful employment of Salmonella.

- Reference: Danzig, R., Sageman, M., Leighton, T. Hough, L., Yuki, H., Kotani, R., Hosford, Z., (2012, Dec). Aum Shinrikyo: Insights into How Terrorists Develop Biological and Chemical Weapons. Second Edition. Center for a New American Security.

- This terrorist group has been able to operate quietly in United States for the last 5 years; systematically preparing for their biological attack. Their scientists have obtained a fatal strain of *Clostridium botulinum*. They have successfully established large-scale fermenter capability, effective storage capability, and a method of dissemination. Additionally, they have multiple cells in all 50 states prepositioned to act simultaneously when directed by the group's leader.

- On August 15, 2014, the terrorist group's leader sends the signal to all cells to initiate the attack. Cells in all 50 states proceed to preselected restaurants with salad bars. Multiple cells in all states target over a thousand salad bars. Hidden on their person is a small finger pump sprayer filled with *Clostridium botulinum*. Cell members dispense the substance in a mist on salad items.

- In Phoenix, Arizona, an alert customer notices a person squirting a substance on the lettuce at a salad bar and alerts the authorities. When the authorities question this person they determine further investigation is needed. They search the suspect and recover the syringe.

Key Questions

- What can or should Law Enforcement do?
- What agencies should be notified?
- What alerts if any should be initiated?

Scenario Day 1 Continued: Authorities determine this was an attempt to contaminate the food on the salad bar. Patrons of the restaurant are requested to standby while LE conducts their investigation. The suspect is not cooperating.

Key Questions

- Should an ICS be stood up? Who will take the lead?
- Who should test the sprayer? What resources are available to provide immediate testing?

The sprayer contents are tested by the State's National Guard WMD team via their mobile lab. It is determined the sprayer contained botulinum toxin.

Key Questions

- What should be done with the restaurant patrons?
- What can LE do to further their investigation despite the suspect not talking?

Federal agencies are immediately notified. Local authorities deem it necessary to establish ICS and an EOC. The media begins to take notice of the escalating response. Alerts begin to filter out to all state's Emergency Centers. Notices are disseminated to be cognizant of similar scenarios at food buffets. There are no other reports from other states or municipalities.

- Authorities are not certain if this is an isolated incident. Based on the fact that it was botulinum, it is considered that a mass quantity was possibly manufactured. The Rajneesh scenario is also considered.
- The EOC directs other food buffets in the Phoenix area should be tested.

Key Questions

- What should be told to the media? What should be withheld? How might they be helpful?
- At this point, what is the federal response expectation?

Scenario Day 1 continued: After testing every restaurant with a buffet line; it was determined 12 of the 16 tested positive for the botulinum toxin. It is determined potentially 1,000 patrons may have been exposed by consuming the food at these locations.

> The EOC with public affairs put together a press briefing. Within the briefing, those potentially exposed are directed to go a central location established to process victims. Despite this, the media's reporting has generated fear within the public. Hospitals within the Phoenix area are beginning to be swarmed with concerned civil populace.

All restaurants with buffets are requested to close. Investigators are systematically going business to business recovering evidence.

Once it was determined that this was not an isolated incident and that 12 restaurants were contaminated, it was determined this should be declared a Public Health Emergency by the Federal Government.

The Phoenix area ICS and EOC is establishing a Joint command to begin accepting the Federal response.

Key Questions

- What federal agencies should be responding? What are their roles?
- What authority exists to shut down private businesses?

Scenario Day 2 continued: It has been 24 hours since the event in Phoenix commenced. Other states are beginning to report small quantities of people reporting being sick with symptoms not normally seen at Urgent Care Centers or Emergency Rooms. Patients are reporting varying types of paralysis in muscles around the head and neck, difficulty swallowing, and respiratory issues. These symptoms are consistent with botulism poisoning. The CDC takes notice and directs a nationwide clinical testing of new patients while simultaneously directing treatment for botulism.

Reference: Botulism Fact Sheet (2014, Feb). UPMC Center for Health Security; www.UPMCHealthsecurity.org

Soon, word spreads via social media. All 50 states are reporting hospitals and Urgent Care Centers being swarmed with concerned citizens.

Hour 32 post-Phoenix, thousands of people are reporting symptoms consistent with botulism poisoning.

Key Questions

- What should the Federal Government do concerning all 50 states reporting illnesses? What type of response is now required?
- What role can the media play? What should the Information Center be doing? What should the message be?
- Is there an antitoxin available? What role does the CDC play for the Nation's ability to counter this type of event?

Scenario Continued: Hour 48 post-Phoenix. At this point, all 50 states are reporting confirmed botulism poisoning. There have been several deaths, mostly with the elderly.

- What resources (Federal) are available for Emergency Managers to develop plans for a response to bioterrorism?

End of scenario: The United States has yet to experience an attack to this scale. Emergency Management often relies on past experiences to build response plans. The closest event to this is the Rajneesh Salmonella poisoning event. There were some lessons learned, but hardly enough to develop full spectrum response to a nationwide event. This scenario was developed to provoke thought on a grandeur scale and generate discussion of what ifs. Occasionally imagining the worst case allows one to prepare for possible inevitabilities.

Hot Wash

- What could have done better?
- What went well?

CHAPTER 8

Tabletop Exercises—Explosive

EXPLOSIVE DEVICE INCIDENT

Applicability and Scope

Tabletop exercises designed for emergency response to terrorism offer opportunities to apply the principles of prevention, protection, mitigation, response, and recovery. Tabletop exercises in the classroom setting provide students the ability to systematically talk through various scenarios. The following

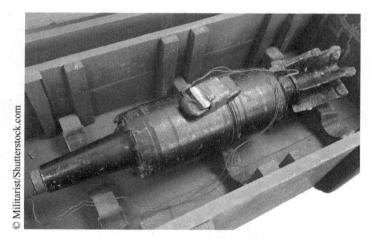

Improvised Explosive Device (IED).

Improvised Explosive Device (IED) scenario should result in conducting an on scene threat assessment to determine the complexity of the incident and the level of response required. This scenario should lead to identify the level of threat, resources needed, protection measures required, mitigation or neutralization options, and recovery requirements. The scope of this exercise is to open discuss with prompts from a moderator's questions.

Purpose

The purpose of this tabletop exercise is to examine current policies, procedures, resources, and actions in the context of an IED incident. This exercise should also promote greater understanding and ability to apply NIMS/ICS principles. This exercise should identify what went well and identify what went wrong in a hot wash setting and result in participants making recommended improvements.

Objectives

The objective of this scenario is to evaluate policies and procedures as outlined in local, state, or federal response plans, to evaluate command and control in the Incident Command construct, and to identify resources needed versus available by applying the concept of on scene threat analysis to determine response requirements. Additional objectives may include identifying response through recovery procedures. The overall objective of this IED scenario is to enhance understanding of the unique dynamics involving the use of IEDs. Participants should extract from this scenario the resources needed to respond to an IED incident, the various diagnostic capabilities, the hazards, mitigation, and recovery requirements. Additionally, participants should have an understanding of how this type of event can escalate to a national-level response and the various agency stakeholders.

- Reference: Homeland Security Exercise and Evaluation Program (2013). Department of Homeland Security, retrieved from https://www.fema.gov/media-library/assets/documents/32326

RULES/CONDUCT

The intent of a tabletop exercise is to create dialogue about various issues in relation to a given scenario. Participants are encouraged to collectively explore in depth the various aspects of the event. Ground rules for a tabletop exercise and open dialogue require creativity and group problem solving. Participants are encouraged to foster active thinking, active listening, and active participation. Most importantly, the group must respect one another, challenge the ideas and not the people. Participants must be encouraged to contribute and understand that there is no admonishment for incorrect decisions.

Tabletops in the classroom generally assume that the following have been met:

- The National Incident Management System implemented
- The municipality has the required resources for response
- The municipality has standard governmental structure
- The affected entity has contingency plans unless the scenario dictates otherwise

ASSIGNMENT OF ROLES

The following are the potential assignment of roles if the standard structure is used. As described in the previous chapter, an alternative structure can be used for teaching purposes.

- Key stakeholders on initial response (first responders):
  - Fire Department:Typically Incident Command
  - Security Forces/Law Enforcement: Establish cordons, initiate evacuations

- Medical:Postblast (if applicable)
  - Key stakeholders follow on response (emergency responders):
  - Explosive Ordnance Disposal (Bomb squad)
  - Public Health (Bioenvironmental)
  - Emergency Management
  - Crime scene investigation (FBI, ATF, State, Local)

- Key stakeholders in the Emergency Operations Center (EOC) (no particular order):
  - EOC Director
  - External Affairs (Media Relations)
  - Search and rescue (accountability of personnel)
  - Public safety
  - Mass care
  - Long-term recovery
  - Logistics
  - Firefighting
  - Public Works
  - Communications (Operational)

- Ancillary stakeholders
  - Community
  - Nongovernmental Organizations
  - Private Sector
  - Local Government
  - State
  - Federal

Reference: National Response Framework, Second Edition,2013May; Department of Homeland Security.

The above identifies potential roles. Not all are necessary for each scenario and additional roles can be added as necessary.

BACKGROUND CONSIDERATIONS FOR AN IED ATTACK

An explosive attack is the most probable of scenarios. An IED is low cost, high impact, easy to obtain resources and to employ. Quite simply, an IED is the most effective method for a terrorist organization to instill fear, disrupt economies, and alter societal norms. Terrorists have repeatedly demonstrated their willingness and ability to use IEDs. This threat should be a priority for Emergency planners when developing action plans with respect to CBRNE.

There are many variables to the employment of an IED. Often there are various stages prior to the use of anIED. Ignoring the motives of the bomber, inherently these stages are fairly consistent with the use of an IED. The first stage to consider is radicalization or cell building; this can consist of a lone wolf or the creation of a complex network of operatives. The next phase includes planning, surveillance, and target selection. Based on the outcome of surveillance and the type of target, the next phase is to construct the device. It is important to note that device construction will have consistent elements that Emergency Planners and responders should be aware of. These elements include the main components of most IEDs. The device will usually have a power source such as a battery. Potentially, the power source can be forgone if the bomber is using a time fuse type initiation. The next component is the initiator such as an electric blasting cap. A switch of some sort is typically used to allow the power to transfer to the electric blasting cap; switches are numerous and can include timers or remote controlled devices such as a cell phone. Finally, the device will have an explosive main charge. The explosives can be homemade or commercially available products like ammonium nitrate. All of these components will typically be consolidated into a container for transport; this could be a vehicle or simply galvanized plumbing pipe. The last phase of IED employment is executing the attack by placing the bomb and detonating the device.

Emergency Planners and responders must be aware of the phases of employment and the elements of device construction. Ensuring that planners and responders are aware of current tactics, techniques and procedures will enhance the overall response capability and substantiate written response plans. Incident commanders should be aware of possible general methods of addressing an IED. Two major methods is to either detonate the bomb where it is (also known as "blow in place") or to render the device safe.

Blow in place is simply to use an explosive charge to detonate the device before it goes off. This procedure is used when the area is clear of all assets and no significant damage is expected. For example, if a device is found at an empty park and there is no possibility that the device will detonate when handled, bomb technicians may present the incident commander with the choice of a blow in place solution. Other situations may arise when the option of a blow in place solution is the best choice. From a bomb technician's perspective, this is the safest option to ensure they face the lowest risk. That said, if the option is not best for the environment, bomb technicians may not even present the possibility of a blow in place.

Rendering the device safe is a procedure to make the bomb safe enough for handling with very little possibility of an inadvertent detonation. The procedures, known as render safe procedures, are classified. The procedures should leave the device safe for handling and transport, but such movements should be limited. Unlike a blow in place, rendering a bomb safe will require the device to be taken to a safe place to dispose of it. Generally, this means taking the device to a place where a detonation of the device can be conducted. Transportation of the device can involve the use of a Total Containment Vessel (TCV) that can withstand a detonation inside of the vessel. Law enforcement may be interested in recovering as much of the device as they can, but this may be in conflict with the wishes of the bomb technicians who would rather not handle the device prior to detonation. After a detonation, either as a blow in place or when detonated at a safe location, evidence can be recovered if bomb technicians clear the residue.

Reference: Subcommittee on Domestic Improvised Explosive Device, (2008 Dec). www.whitehouse.gov
Reference: Subcommittee on Domestic Improvised Explosive Device, (2008Dec). www.whitehouse.gov

Case Studies to Review: Case studies that deserve review are the Boston bombing and the Oklahoma City bombing. These cases illustrate the process previously discussed. Both cases demonstrate the radicalization, planning, surveillance, target selection, construct the device, and attack execution phases. These two cases also highlight the other elements of material acquisition, high impact, and ease of employment.

The 117th running of the Boston Marathon occurred on April 15, 2013. This race draws thousands of participants and spectators. The race coincides with the state of Massachusetts celebrating Patriot's Day; a day to reflect on patriotism and independence. At 2:49 p.m., near the race finish line, two IEDs detonated amidst spectator viewing areas. Post blast investigation revealed that these devices were pressure

© Hang Dinh/Shutterstock.com

A makeshift memorial for the Boston Marathon bombing victims.

cooker design and filled with low explosives and shrapnel. The devices were emplaced hidden inside backpacks. The IED designs mirrored devices in the Al-Qaeda's Inspire magazine. The magazine emphasized this type of device as it is to acquire materials and construct. The Boston Marathon indicates careful target selection; targeted was a significant American ideal being celebrated (Patriot's Day) and a high-impact event where many casualties would result.

Investigation revealed the suspects, DzhokharTsarnaev and his brother TamerlanTsarnaev had been downloading propagandist materials. Much of the material was authored by Anwar Al-Awlaki, a well-known Al-Qaeda operative. This material heavily influenced their belief that violent jihad was required to avenge perceived wrong doings against Muslims. During this phase of self-radicalization; investigation showed the brothers began to plan an attack. They acquired materials for their IED's and also various weapons and ammunition. Most of the material they acquired was readily available for purchase online or through a vendor. Device construction was relatively easy as the Inspire magazine provided step-by-step instructions. The brothers employed their devices on April 15, 2013, and detonated the IEDs in crowded viewing areas; this resulted in the deaths of three people, and injuring over 200 others.

This case study reveals the phases of attack formulation: self-radicalization by Al-Qaeda propaganda, attack planning by acquiring materials and target selection, device construction using step-by-step guide in Inspire magazine, and IED employment concealed in backpacks and attack execution.

Reference: United States of America v. Dzhokhar A. Tsarnaev Indictment, http://www.fbi .gov/news/updates-on-investigation-into-multiple-explosions-in-boston

The second case study that demonstrates the phases of an IED attack is the Oklahoma City bombing of the Murrah Federal Building. The perpetrators of this event included three main suspects: Timothy McVeigh, Terry Nichols, and Michael Fortier. McVeigh and Nichols met each other in Army basic training. Fortier was befriended a few years before the bombing. This group came together by having a similar hatred toward the federal government. McVeigh encouraged all his acquaintances to read a book called the *Turner Diaries* that encouraged violence against the federal government. This group perceived that the federal government was suppressing constitutional rights. A significant catalyst for their violent radicalization was the federal government raids of Ruby Ridge and the Branch Davidians compound. Significantly, April 19, 1993, the federal government raided the Davidian's compound resulting in 74 men, women, and children being killed in a massive fire believed to have been started by devices fired by the federal agents. In May 1993, McVeigh, Fortier, and Nichols began conspiring to attack federal government targets. From May 1993 through Dec 1994, the three individuals acquire the various materials needed to construct a vehicle borne IED (VBIED).

Some material such as ammonium nitrate and nitromethane are purchased, some material such as high-explosive boosters and blasting caps are stolen. By January 1995, after much surveillance, McVeigh had selected his target in Oklahoma City. In March 1995, Nichols backs out of the plot. In early April 1995, Fortier backs out of the plot. In and around April 17, 1995, McVeigh proceeds with the plan and begins to finalize construction of the VBIED. He rents a Ryder truck and loads the back with explosives. On April 19, 1995, he drives the Ryder truck to the Murrah Federal Building, lights time fuse, parks the truck in front of the building, and walks away to a prestaged getaway car. At 9:02 a.m., over 2 tons of ammonium nitrate mixed with nitromethane detonates destroying most of the Murrah building. One hundred fifty-seven people died and over five hundred injured.

The Oklahoma City national memorial.

This case study also highlights the phases of an IED attack. They were self-radicalized by various national events, and association with individuals with like-minded ideologies. Next, they thoroughly planned, surveyed, and selected a high-impact target. Finally, the device was constructed and executed in an attack.

Reference: Famous Trials, Oklahoma City Bombing Trial (Timothy McVeigh) http://law2 .umkc.edu/faculty/projects/ftrials/mcveigh/mcveightrial.html

TABLETOP SCENARIO OVERVIEW

Due to world events and several incidents occurring in Canada, the Department of Homeland Security has begun to issue terrorist threat summaries more frequently. There has been a significant emphasis on having situational awareness on public transit. In light of previous successful attacks in Madrid, Spain, there has been a renewed urgency to plan for terrorist events related to public transportation such as buses and subways.

Key Questions

- What can Emergency Planners do to prepare their areas of responsibility for these renewed terrorist scenarios?
- What should state and local agencies be doing?
- What role do the media play? How can they be used to message this alert?

RESUMPTION OF SCENARIO

The United States' heavy involvement engaging the Islamic State in Iraq and Syria has resulted in the leaders within this organization to call on all Muslim followers to conduct jihad within the United States. Their intent is to take advantage of social media outlets and influence lone wolfs to self-radicalize. Radical Internet forums are full of chatter and the dissemination of online magazines such as Al-Qaeda's Inspire. The most recent Inspire discusses heavily how to attack public buses by providing advice on what type of device to use, where to get explosives, and how to emplace an IED on board a bus.

Key Questions

- How would Emergency Planners involve the private sector concerning these renewed threats?
- What responsibility does the private sector have concerning material acquisition?
- What precautions should public transit be taking?
- Given the Boston Bombing case study, how plausible is an attack on public transit?
- Give examples where material for an IED can be obtained. How hard are the materials to obtain?
- What can Emergency Responders do to prepare for these renewed threats? Fire Department? Medical? Law Enforcement? Bomb Squad? Who else?

SCENARIO CONTINUED

A small cell with radical Islamic ideology has taken notice of the U.S. attacks of Muslims in the newly formed Islamic State. The U.S. air campaign has generated enormous resentment toward the United States. This cell has approximately 10 members. They routinely meet to discuss world events and share propaganda. Their most recent meeting has focused on the call to jihad from the leaders of the new Islamic State. They all agree that it is their duty to conduct attacks against the United States. During their discussions, they review Al-Qaeda's

Inspire tactics suggesting attacks on public transit. The 10 members decide to expand this to attacking several different venues, including buses, malls, and busy restaurants. Their plan requires these venues to be attacked simultaneously to ensure the most success and create the most panic and fear. They have chosen 10 targets, one for each member. The next phase for the cell is to survey their potential targets.

Key Questions

- Considering the advanced warning from DHS, how can Emergency Planners ensure the public has situational awareness?
- What should the public be informed to look for?
- What could lead to this cell's plan being discovered before they have the opportunity to execute it?

SCENARIO CONTINUED

The 10 members of the cell spend the next 2 weeks surveying their chosen targets. They have decided to target two malls (food courts), the main public bus lines in downtown (three buses total), and five heavily patronized restaurants. The cell decides to meet to discuss the type of devices they will use to execute their attacks. Reviewing past successful attacks, they deemed pipe bombs as easy to obtain the material and to construct. The cell makes a list of required materials and sets out to acquire the resources needed to build dozens of pipe bombs.

Key Questions

- What role does the private sector have in suspicious purchases?
- Where can Emergency Planners or other stakeholders obtain up to date information on threats and intelligence?
- How can the private sector be informed of increased threats and what to look for?
- Research what explosive materials are regulated by the federal government.

SCENARIO CONTINUED

The cell eventually acquired the material they needed. To avoid suspicion, they separated their purchases into small quantities and spread their purchases across dozens of vendors. They drove to multiple different sporting goods stores to purchase smokeless powder. They also purchased small quantities of fireworks at various different vendors; the remainder of their supplies was ordered online.

With the successful acquisition of their supplies, the cell meets to construct their devices. They have decided to "daisy chain" five pipe bombs and conceal them in backpacks. Each bomber will have one backpack with five pipe bombs designed to simultaneously detonate. The cell has chosen to use galvanized pipe supplemented with ball bearings as shrapnel. Their triggering mechanism is a "throw away" cell phone. Their fusing is electric squibs obtained from multiple hobby stores.

With their devices constructed, the cell is ready to employ their IEDs. To raise the impact of their attack, they decide to attack on a significant date. They chose September 11 as their attack date.

The cell disperses to their targets. They decide 12:00 p.m. will be their time for all members to initiate their devices. Buses will have passengers during the lunch rush hour, the mall food courts will be packed with patrons just as their chosen restaurants will be busy.

Each cell member disperses to their targets. The three cell members targeting the downtown bus lines successfully emplace their backpacks under a bus seat. The cell members targeting the two malls find seats in the food courts and patiently wait for the noon hour. The cell members targeting restaurants are in place and will simply walk away from their table a couple of minutes before noon.

As the noon hour approaches, one of the cell members at the first mall food court sits at a table. Five minutes to noon, he begins to walk away leaving his backpack in place. An attentive mall security guard notices the man leaving his personal belongings and confronts the man. The cell member panics and runs from the guard. Suspecting an IED, the guard begins evacuating the food court and notifies the mall command post to call 911 about a suspect backpack.

At 11:55, the police are notified and the single municipality bomb squad is dispatched to the mall.

At 11:58, the cell members dispersed to the restaurants are in place, a couple of minutes before noon they calmly walk away from their tables.

At 12:00 noon, the backpacks placed on the three downtown buses detonate. The first calls to 911 are providing different and confusing information. All that is known is there are multiple detonations with many dead and injured.

Within a minute of the first 911 calls from downtown, there are new 911 calls from three area restaurants that have had bombs detonate inside the restaurants. Witnesses on scene are reporting dozens injured and many dead.

At 12:04, the second mall targeted has a suspect backpack reported to security. Security evacuates the food court and requests response for emergency services via 911.

At 12:05, there are 911 calls from two restaurants about patrons leaving a backpack and walking away. They have heard of news reports about detonations in the city, and find this suspicious as the patrons have abandoned their bags and departed the area. A waiter opened one of the backpacks reports seeing pipe bombs. Both restaurants are evacuated.

At 12:07, the bomb squad arrives where they were originally dispatched (the first mall). Hearing the radio traffic, they ascertain there are multiple detonation scenes and also additional suspect devices.

To recap, there have been three detonations downtown on buses with multiple dead and injured. There are 911 calls from three area restaurants reporting multiple dead and injured. There are 911 calls from two restaurants reporting suspect backpacks and two 911 calls from malls reporting suspect backpacks. In total, there are six reported detonations and four reported suspect backpacks.

Key Questions

- What is the first priority of emergency responders?
  - What should the fire department be doing? Law enforcement? Bomb Squad? Medical responders?
- What hazards could be present to responders?
- Considering there are multiple scenes, how will responses be prioritized?
- If the municipality resources are overwhelmed, where can additional resources come from?
- What type of command system should be established?
- Who is in charge when there are 10 different response scenes?
- Is it too early in the incident to establish media relations? What should the message be?
- What should be the national-level response? Should the terror alert level be increased?

SCENARIO CONTINUED

News reports are numerous; there is much speculation and misinformation. The municipality is overwhelmed as more 911 calls are pouring in. Concerned citizens are reporting dozens of suspect packages. Panic is immense within the city; many roads are closed by law enforcement, businesses are beginning to close for the day, and schools are in lock down. Frightened parents are trying to gain access to their children.

Key Questions

- What role does the public affairs representative have? How can the panic be tamed?

SCENARIO CONTINUED

At 12:15, the city Emergency Management recommends establishing a Unified Command, standing up the EOC and immediately requesting additional resources by activating support agreements and mutual aid agreements.

Key Questions

- What elements make up the Unified Command system?
- What elements make up the EOC?
- What resources are immediately needed?
- Given 10 incident scenes, would it be prudent to have 10 Incident Management Teams reporting to the UC?
- Should an Area Command be established? What type of command is more beneficial?
- What role do elected and appointed city officials have?

SCENARIO CONTINUED

As the command system is being worked out, individual incident scenes are currently being managed by the first Fire Department IC on scene. It is quickly becoming apparent, the city does not have enough ambulance resources; the three areas hospitals are overwhelmed. Medical officials are triaging. All off duty physicians are being recalled.

At 12:30, the first EOC members are trickling in; the EOC's main reporting location is City Hall, the city council's chambers are dual purpose and also serve the EOC. The Unified Command is forming at the city's main fire station.

At 12:30, the two mall food courts and the two restaurants are evacuated. The Bomb Squad is still on scene at the first mall; they are awaiting prioritization before beginning any operations. There have been several calls for their service as there are a total of six detonation scenes, four known suspect backpacks, and a dozen or so additional calls to 911 of other suspect packages.

Key Questions

- Since there is currently only one Bomb Squad, what should be the priority?
- Where can the city obtain immediate additional Bomb Squad resources?
- What agencies are available to assist with Bomb Squad resources?

- Under what circumstances can the Department of Defense resources be requested?
- How can the other suspect package scenes be expeditiously cleared to lessen the burden on emergency services

SCENARIO CONTINUED

The Unified Command has fully stood up. The main stake holders are in place and are funneling requests to the EOC. The EOC is vigorously working to obtain additional resources. Federal agencies are beginning to show up offering assistance; the UC is requesting lead federal representative's report to their location at the main fire station.

At 12:35, the UC determines to redirect the Bomb Squad to the bus detonation scenes. Since the two malls and restaurants are evacuated, they feel those scenes can stay cordoned off and respond to them later. They want the bus scenes cleared for any additional hazards that may endanger the first responders.

At 12:40, the Bomb Squad arrives on scene of one of the bus detonations. Information is passed to the Bomb Squad that there is an undetonated pipe bomb in the wreckage of the bus.

The scene still has several dead personnel; the injured have been evacuated from the immediate area.

Key Questions

- Given the scene being evacuated, should the pipe bomb be a concern?
- What is the cordon required for a standard 12-inch pipe bomb? (Reference: ATF Bomb Evacuation Distances)
- What should the Bomb Squad do?

SCENARIO CONTINUED

The Bomb Squad informs the IC to keep the area cordoned off and to not allow personnel to enter the area. The Bomb Squad proceeds to the next bus scene.

At 12:50, they arrive on scene. This scene is still chaotic, due to a lack of ground evacuation resources there are still injured personnel in the vicinity of the damaged bus. There are reported eight personnel dead. The IC for this incident reports not seeing any additional hazards. The Bomb Squad quickly surveys the scene looking for secondary devices and any other explosive hazards; they declare the scene safe.

At 13:00, the Bomb Squad arrives the third bus scene; the IC has ensured all personnel are clear of the bus wreckage. A quick survey reveals no hazards.

At 1:10, the Unified Command notifies the Bomb Squad commander that additional Bomb Squad resources have arrived. The nearby military installation was requested and was able to provide two teams.

Incident Commanders at the 10 sites have reported their dead, injured, and missing. So far, there are 45 dead, 406 injured, and missing is to be determined.

There are still injured at the detonation sites requiring medical attention. The most severely injured have been transported to medical facilities.

At 1:15, the EOC is reported to be fully operational. The Unified Command is reported to have the main stakeholders with a representative present.

Additional medical support is also trickling in from outside agencies and nearby municipalities.

Key Questions

- What is the immediate priority?
- Considering the additional Bomb Squad support, what should now be the priority for the Bomb Squad teams?
- What other resources are going to be needed?
  - Medical? Civil Engineering? Transportation?
- How will the dead be processed?
- How will the crime scenes be processed?
  - When will the crime scenes be processed?
  - Who has the lead on the crime scenes?
  - What resources are needed to process the scene?
- What should the UC and EOC be planning for?

SCENARIO CONTINUED

The Unified Command directs medical resources to the scenes with injured on site. Some will be transported to outside the area hospitals. Transportation is being arranged via the EOC for large volume transport of injured personnel.

The Bomb Squad teams have been directed to the three remaining detonation scenes at the restaurants. Each site receives a team. The teams clear the detonation sites for secondary devices and additional explosive hazards and are standing by for their next assignments.

At 2:00, it has been determined to issue a press release.

Key Questions

- Where should the Bomb Squads be dispatched next?
- Who coordinates transportation requirements? Where can they obtain additional resources?
- What should the press release say?

SCENARIO CONTINUED

The UC dispatches one Bomb Squad team to the undetonated pipe bomb at the bus scene. Another team is dispatched to mall number 1 and the third Bomb Squad team is dispatched to mall number 2.

The Bomb Squad at the bus scene successfully removes the pipe bomb with a robot and places it in their TCV. They did not want to destroy it so that evidence can be obtained from it. They transport it from the scene to a safe location and perform a render safe procedure. The local FBI Special Agent Bomb Technician (SABT) accompanies the Bomb Squad to facilitate evidence collection.

The Bomb Squads dispatched to the mall scenes begin their procedures. Both teams deploy robots for initial reconnaissance. These backpack devices did not detonate for some reason and the intelligence to be gathered from them is critical.

Key Questions

- What evidence can be obtained from the devices?
- How can this evidence or device construction be critical? Who needs this information?

SCENARIO CONTINUED

The Bomb Squads at the mall scenes have completed their diagnostics and have determined that the switching mechanism (cell phones) has failed to initiate the squibs. The teams complete their render safe procedures and transfer the evidence to the FBI.

The Unified Command dispatches two Bomb Squads to the area restaurants with remaining backpacks. The same diagnostics reveal the cell phones failed to initiate the squibs. Again, the evidence is turned over to the FBI.

Key Questions

- Now that all the unexploded devices are rendered safe, what should the next priority be?
- How can the UC reduce the number of false reporting on suspect packages? What information can be provided to the public to facilitate package identification as suspect or not?

SCENARIO CONTINUED

At 4:00, the injured have all been evacuated and are being treated in various hospitals. There are still dead personnel on scene that have not been removed yet.

Federal and state resources are arriving.

Key Questions

- Concerning the command construct, what should they be doing at this phase of the incident?
- Who will provide infrastructure repair?
- What Presidential declaration can facilitate additional resources and funding? Does this event qualify?

Hot Wash

- What could have been done better?
- What went well?

Websites for further study and information:
https://www.llis.dhs.gov/

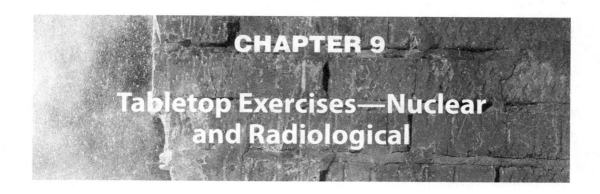

CHAPTER 9

Tabletop Exercises—Nuclear and Radiological

NUCLEAR/RADIOLOGICAL INCIDENT

Applicability and Scope

Tabletop exercises designed for emergency response to terrorism offer opportunities to apply the principles of prevention, protection, mitigation, response, and recovery. Tabletop exercises in the classroom setting provide students the ability to systematically talk through various scenarios. The following radiological scenario should result in conducting an on scene threat assessment to determine the complex-

Nuclear explosion.

ity of the incident and the level of response required. This scenario should lead to identifying the level of threat, resources needed, protection measures required, mitigation or neutralization options, and recovery requirements. The scope of this exercise is to open discuss with prompts from a moderator's questions.

Purpose

The purpose of this tabletop exercise is to examine current policies, procedures, resources and actions in the context of a radiological incident. This exercise should also promote greater understanding and ability to apply NIMS/ICS principles. This exercise should identify what went well and identify what went wrong in a hot wash setting and result in participants making recommended improvements.

Consideration for this tabletop exercise should be given to the intent vice the actual plausibility or effectiveness of a radiological attack. The purpose of this tabletop is to exercise the response to a national-level event, not dispute whether or not it could actually happen. Every attempt was made to ensure certain levels of realism and preserve certain levels of plausibility.

LEARNING OUTCOMES

1. Evaluate policies and procedures as outlined in local, state, or federal response plans

2. Evaluate command and control in the Incident Command construct

3. Identify resources needed versus available by applying the concept of on scene threat analysis to determine response requirements

4. Identifying response through recovery procedures

5. Enhance understanding of the unique dynamics involving the use of radiological materials

Participants should extract from this scenario that the resources needed to respond to a radiological incident, the various detection capabilities, the hazards, mitigation, and recovery requirements. Additionally, participants should have an understanding how this type of event will escalate to a National-level response and the various agency stakeholders.

- Reference: Homeland Security Exercise and Evaluation Program (2013). Department of Homeland Security, retrieved from https://www.fema.gov/media-library/assets/documents/32326

Rules/Conduct

The intent of a tabletop exercise is to create dialogue about various issues in relation to a given scenario. Participants are encouraged to collectively explore in depth the various aspects of the event. Ground rules for a tabletop exercise and open dialogue require creativity and group problem solving. Participants are encouraged to foster active thinking, active listening, and active participation. Most importantly, the group must respect one another, challenge the ideas and not the people. Participants must be encouraged to contribute and understand that there is no admonishment for incorrect decisions.

Tabletops in the classroom generally assume that the following have been met:

- National Incident Management System implemented
- Municipality has the required resources for response
- Municipality has standard governmental structure
- Affected entity has contingency plans unless the scenario dictates otherwise

- Assignment of Roles:
- Key stake holders on initial response (first responders):
  - Fire Department: Typically Incident Command
  - Security Forces/Law Enforcement: Establish cordons, initiate evacuations
  - Medical
- Key stake holders on follow on response (emergency responders):
  - Explosive Ordnance Disposal (Bomb Squad)
  - Public Health (Bioenvironmental)
  - Emergency Management
  - Crime scene investigation (FBI)
- Key stake holders in the Emergency Operations Center (EOC)
  - EOC Director
  - Public affairs (Media Relations)
  - Search and rescue (accountability of personnel)
  - Public safety
  - Long-term recovery
  - Logistics
  - Firefighting
  - Communications
- Other roles as necessary

BACKGROUND CONSIDERATIONS FOR A RADIOLOGICAL ATTACK

Radiological attacks should be framed in the context of "radiation dispersion." A nuclear device is obviously more dynamic and includes additional destruction parameters such as expansive blast, gamma effects, and the spread of radiation fallout potentially out to hundreds of miles. For the purpose of this tabletop scenario, the focus is strictly on the use of radiological material incorporated into a dispersion device with the terms radio-logical dispersion device (RDD) and "dirty bomb" being used interchangeably. The U.S. Nuclear Regulatory Commission offers this definition of a "dirty bomb," "type of a radiological dispersal device that combines conventional explosives, such as dynamite, with radioactive material" (NRC Fact Sheet, 2012). However, it must be considered that radiation can potentially be employed in other methods. Depending on the material, it is possible to simply place a sufficient quantity in one area resulting in an exposure threat to bystanders. The result of this exposure is acute radiation sickness. Material may also be disseminated via other methods such as manually spread by introducing powdered material to ventilation systems or simply dispensed from a tall office building. Ulti-mately, radiation exposure can occur via three pathways: gamma, beta, and alpha parti-cles deposited on the surface of the skin and inhalation of suspended material (NRC Fact Sheet, 2012). Emergency planners and responders must consider all dissemination and exposure possibilities. The following exercise is intended to provoke thought and discus-sion based on a national-level crisis. One must consider the method of deployment of radiological material. If an organization makes the investment to obtain the material and develop a dispersion method, then the sophistication and complexity of the device must be considered.

Case Studies to Review: A couple of case studies deserve review. Of note, the case studies revolve around proliferation of material and accidental exposures; there are no known suc-cessful terrorist uses of RDD's.

The first case study demonstrates how simple exposure to a static source can inflict sig-nificant damage. On September 13, 1987, in Goiania, Brazil, cesium-137 chloride was removed from a teletherapy machine. Scrappers removed the source from its sealed container and unknowingly exposed the town to the effects of cesium as the material was passed around. Forty-nine people were hospitalized, 5 died, 85 buildings contaminated, and 7 had to be destroyed. The importance of this event demonstrates two essential elements: (1) Source material availability and (2) the extent of damage a static exposure can inflict (Hudley, Charlton, & Childress, 2010).

The second case study involves cesium-137 in Russia. In 1995 November, Chechen rebels notified a television news station about a Radiation Dispersal Device they had planted in Moscow's Izmailovsky Park. It was determined that the device was an explosive RDD using dynamite. It is estimated the package weighed 32 kg containing 50 mCi of cesium-137 removed from a hospital X-ray machine. The device did not explode and was recovered by authorities. Many details from this incident are unknown; however, this highlights a terrorist organization's intent and the capacity to obtain a source and build a bomb.

SCENARIO OVERVIEW

A recent publication of Al-Qaeda's Inspire discussed that various tactics lone wolves could employ in the continental United States. One topic revolved around the use of radioactive materials in a dirty bomb scenario. The article proceeded to highlight various open source information outlets and how sources could be obtained. The article provided techniques for dispensing the radiation including using explosives or possibly deploying it in a static mode where the public would be exposed to external radiation.

Key Questions

- What would be the main results of using an RDD? Why would terrorists choose this unconventional method?
- Where could terrorists obtain source material? What would make the best material for an RDD?
- What is the difference between a nuclear device and a radiation dispersal device? What is similar?
- What should Emergency Planners and responders do in reaction to increased threats of terrorist use of RDD's?
- Who validates the threat? Where would state and local agencies receive their information?

RESUMPTION OF SCENARIO

A terrorist cell that has been operating on a low-scale extracts many tactics from Al-Qaeda's Inspire. This cell has decided to act on the recommendations to use a radiation dispersal device. This cell operates in the Colorado Springs, Colorado area and has only conducted small-scale events in the past. Unknown to authorities, they have been responsible for the frequent forest fires every summer for the last 4 years. This tactic was also introduced in the Al-Qaeda's Inspire magazine. This particular cell is low key and only has four members. Their leader has decided to intensify their contribution to the Al-Qaeda ideology in response to U.S. involvement in the Middle-East. This cell views being the first terrorist group to successfully employ a RDD as a great achievement and will garner substantial recognition for Al-Qaeda.

Key Questions

- Is it possible that terrorist acts go unnoticed by authorities?
- Are they merely misclassified or intentionally not labeled terrorist acts?

- What role does the federal government play in monitoring published threats to the United States?
- Should state and local agencies act on threats despite the federal government down-playing or not validating the threat?
- Who determines an act is classified as terrorism?

SCENARIO CONTINUED

Using open source data on the Internet, the terrorist cell begins their research to identify the best methods to obtain radioactive sources and explosives. They determine there are multiple methods, but concede theft is the best method to stay unnoticed. Their planning phase begins with determining where the main components, explosives, and radiation source can be stolen. Again, using open source Internet files, they are able identify licensed explosive storage locations and licensed radioactive source locations. Using this information, they formulate a plan to steal both components simultaneously. The terrorist cell also discusses what their target will be. They have determined that the military targets in the area are too complicated to gain access. However, through reconnaissance, they have identified a military base with key components close to the perimeter with civilian access. Realizing the political and economic impact of being able to successfully contaminate a military installation, they commence with a plan to exploit the vulnerability of being close to the perimeter.

Key Questions

- For the student: research Government Accounting Office (GAO) reports on protection of radioactive sources.
  - Based on your findings:
- How can sources be obtained?
- Has radiation source security been improved since the GAO reports have been published?
- What are the key components of terrorist planning?

SCENARIO CONTINUED

Executing their plan, the terrorist cell identifies a veterinary clinic that has a cesium-137 source in one of their diagnostic machines. Additionally, they identify a remote privately owned tactical training school that has high explosives stored on site in small ATF-approved bunkers. They also assume that blasting cap initiators will be in one of the bunkers. Since they have a target identified, they must develop a method how to deploy their RDD. Looking back at some Irish

Republican Army tactics, they identified a technique where a homemade mortar system may be the best method. They decide to copy the Mk 15 Barrack Buster concept.

This concept is composed of a modified gas cylinder tank into a mortar tube and placed on a launch platform. The terrorist cell decides to mount their launch tube in the back of an old pickup truck they acquired. These preparations were completed before the theft of the main components. Their plan consists of loading the tube with their RDD and launching their device via an expelling charge. Their goal is to have the device explode above the critical military facilities increasing the spread of radiation.

After conducting reconnaissance, they determine that they can separate into two teams and steal the explosives and radiation components at the same time. Stealing the components simultaneously reduces the risk in security being increased before they can steal the second component. The cell was successful at breaking into both facilities and retrieved the desired components. They hastily construct their RDD by encasing the radiation source capsule in 15 pounds of explosives and attaching a preassembled timing device designed to detonate the blasting caps within a few seconds after leaving the mortar tube. With their device assembled, they are ready to execute the next phase.

Key Questions

- What are the hazards of cesium-137?
- What is the typical source strength of medical sources?
- Would the terrorists be exposed to radiation?
- What are the symptoms of radiation exposure?

SCENARIO CONTINUED

The terrorist cell loads their modified mortar system with their constructed RDD and proceeds to their attack point. They park their pickup truck near the perimeter where civilians can gain access and aim their mortar RDD at the military facilities. They use a timing system to allow opportunity to escape. Five minutes go by and the mortar ignites expelling the RDD into the air. The device successfully detonates above the critical military facilities.

Key Questions

- If detonated in the air, how would contamination spread?
- What tools are available to responders to plot the hazard?
- Since this event encompasses both civilian property and Department of Defense property, who takes the lead ICS functions?

- What responders are needed?
- Would the truck and remaining mortar tube still be suspicious?

SCENARIO CONTINUED

Military officials on the base hear the detonation. Personnel near the detonation witness seeing a detonation similar to a firework exploding. Security forces respond and begin to establish cordons. The facilities are directed to evacuate. Unknowingly, several hundred personnel exit through the contamination. The fire department establishes Incident Command. They identify an entry control point. As the fire department is establishing the safe zone, radiation detectors worn by responders begin to ring off. Using more advanced detectors, fire department personnel realize that there is significant radioactive contamination.

Key Questions

- What should be done with the personnel that evacuated?
- What should the ICS do in relation to their safe area?
- What personal protective equipment should be worn at this stage?
- What types of tools are available to identify the radiation and extent of contamination?
- Who should the ICS request to immediately respond?
- How would the civilian authorities be absorbed into this response?

SCENARIO CONTINUED

- The ICS directs personnel to wear appropriate PPE. They move the ICS safe area, but are themselves contaminated. The ICS directs all personnel previously evacuated to a staging area outside the main radiation plume, preliminary scans determine several hundred personnel are contaminated on clothes, skin, and possibly by ingestion.
- The military base has directed it be placed in Force Protection Condition Delta which results in extensive security measures and restricted movement of nonessential personnel due to a terrorist attack (AFI 10-245, 2012).
- The ICS requests a joint EOC to be established with the local municipality per standing Support Agreements.

- The ICS requests additional military emergency responders; Explosive Ordnance Disposal (EOD), Bioenvironmental and Emergency Management.
- A second ICS is established by civilian authorities on the city property in proximity to the abandoned vehicle. The vehicle and its contents are being treated as suspicious until cleared by their municipality bomb squad.

Key Questions

- How can two separate ICS ensure coordination with one another?
- How do military services adopt National incident Management System and Incident Command Systems? How do their Support Functions correlate to NIMS and ICS?
- What is the construct of a joint EOC with military and civilian agencies?
- What should the military ICS be planning for?
- What role and capabilities do military EOD, Bioenvironmental and Emergency Management have?
- This has been considered as an obvious terrorist attack; what federal agencies must be notified?
  - How are other federal agencies notified? Is there a single point of contact to initiate notification across all stake holders?
- What other response capabilities are available for the ICS if requested?
  - Federal?
  - Military?
- Under the National Response Framework and National Incident Management System, what is the command structure when factoring military, federal, state, and local agencies?
- What type of Public Affairs statement should be released? What role does the Joint Information Center play in media and public relations?

SCENARIO CONTINUED

- The event is still in the early stages. Both military and civilian ICS are still managing prevention of loss of life, additional property damage, and conducting searches for secondary threats. The joint EOC is up and functioning, and various federal agencies are filtering in with their preliminary representatives. Initial notification has gone out from the military base to the National Military Command Center (NMCC) (AFI 10-206,

2011). Civilian authorities have also made appropriate notifications. Up channeling the incident has resulted in all federal stake holders being notified.

- The civilian ICS is in control of the abandoned vehicle scene. Their responding bomb squad has completed reconnaissance of the vehicle and declares the scene safe from explosive hazards. The ICS clears the area for any radiation hazards and determines zero readings in their area. The ICS transitions into maintaining the scene as a crime scene. The FBI is anxious to gain access to the abandoned vehicle to begin processing for evidence. The FBI has also connected the recent explosive and radioactive source theft to the current incident.

- The military ICS has established its cold, warm, and hot zones. The fire department has stood up its hazmat decontamination line. The ICS and EOC are formulating plans to process all personnel contaminated. The EOD team has surveyed the area and identified no additional explosive hazards. The EOD team has also marked as evidence fragments and debris presumed to be from the RDD. Bioenvironmental has identified the isotope as cesium-137. Emergency Management (EM) has plotted the plume and identified the contaminated area. EM has determined approximately 5 acres including three critical military command centers are in the contamination zone. The ICS decides to vacate the hot and warm zones and process the first responders and emergency responders out of the area. It is determined that there are many vehicles contaminated along with many pieces of emergency response equipment. These equipment items are abandoned in the hot zone.

Key Questions

- What potential evidence can the FBI ascertain from the abandoned vehicle?

- What can be garnered from the debris and fragments suspected to be from the RDD?

- How can the several hundred personnel that are potentially contaminated be processed and decontaminated?

- What resources will the military ICS need to make this happen? What federal resources are available? Any specialized teams?

- How will their health be monitored? What medical professionals are needed?

- How will the FBI process the contaminated evidence?

END OF SCENARIO

- The ICS has determined the immediate threat is over. However, there is the residual threat of radioactive contamination. It is recommended for the base to downgrade Force Protection Delta to a lesser posture of Force Protection Charlie which is implemented when some form of terrorism against the base is likely (AFI 10-245, 2012).
- The joint EOC and military ICS decide to meet to determine the way forward. Significant issues determined that need to be addressed: cleanup of contamination, health monitoring, recovery of critical command elements inside the hot zone such as communication equipment, and relocation of the operations that were conducted within the critical facilities.

Key Questions

- What case studies can be referenced for the likely hood of a successful cleanup?
- What federal agencies provide expertise to cleanup of radioactive incidents?
- What impact will this have across the Department of Defense?
- What are the political ramifications?

Hot Wash

- What could have been done better?
- What went well?

References

- Air Force Instruction 10-245 (2012 September). ANTITERRORISM. Retrieved from http://www.e-publishing.af.mil/index.asp
- Air Force Instruction 10-206 (2011 September). OPERATIONAL REPORTING. Retrieved from http://www.e-publishing.af.mil/index.asp

INDEX